£ 9.5

CW00960583

STOMA CARE

A guide for nurses, doctors and
other health care workers

Titles of related interest, from Beaconsfield Publishers Ltd

Behavioural Science in Medicine
Helen Winefield, PhD and Marilyn Peay, PhD
357 pages, limp and cased, 1980.   Comprehensive introduction to behavioural science for students of medicine and post-registration nursing. Co-published with Allen & Unwin Ltd.

Nursing and Midwifery Sourcebook
Arnold Lancaster, MSc, RGN, SCM, RNT
304 pages, limp, 1979.   Detailed information on the UK institutions and organisations that directly affect the daily work and personal careers of nurses and midwives. Co-published with Allen & Unwin Ltd.

Take Care of Your Elderly Relative
Dr Muir Gray, MD, MB, ChB, DPH and Heather McKenzie, LLB
208 pages, limp and cased, 1980.   Highly successful A to Z of how to care for a dependent elderly person. Much practical advice, both for the lay person and the health care professional. Co-published with Allen & Unwin Ltd.

In preparation
The Home Care of a Dying and Disabled Relative
Professor Eric Wilkes, FRCP, FRCGP, OBE

The Nursing Care of the Dying Patient
Alison Charles-Edwards, SRN, HVCert., JBCNSCert. (Terminal Care)

Stoma Care

A guide for nurses, doctors and
other health care workers

Edited by

Brigid Breckman

SRN, RSCN, JBCNS Certificate in
Stoma Care, DipN(Lond)

Stoma care nurse, Royal Marsden Hospital, London

Foreword by Baroness McFarlane of Llandaff
Professor of Nursing, University of Manchester

BEACONSFIELD PUBLISHERS
Beaconsfield, Bucks, England

First published in 1981

This book is copyright under the Berne Convention. All rights are reserved. Apart from any fair dealing for the purpose of private study, research, criticism or review, as permitted under the Copyright Act 1956, no part of this publication may be reproduced, stored in a retrieval system, or transmitted, in any form or by any means, electronic, electrical, chemical, mechanical, optical, photocopying, recording or otherwise, without the prior permission of the copyright owner. Enquiries should be addressed to the Publishers at 20 Chiltern Hills Road, Beaconsfield, Bucks HP9 1PL, England.

© Beaconsfield Publishers Ltd 1981

British Library Cataloguing in Publication Data

Stoma Care.
   1. Enterostomy
   2. Postoperative care
   I. Breckman, Brigid
   617'.533   RD540

   ISBN 0–906584–04–3

Line illustrations by R. Thornton, BA (Hons),
Trent House, Sherborne, Dorset, England.

Typeset in 10 on 12 point Times (C.A.T.),
printed and bound in Great Britain
by Billing and Sons Limited,
Guildford, London, Oxford, Worcester.

To our husbands

Foreword

by Professor Baroness McFarlane of Llandaff

The identification of clinical specialties in nursing has been one of the responsibilities of the Joint Board of Clinical Nursing Studies since its inception in 1970. Stoma Care nursing was so recognised in 1973 and a curriculum developed for registered nurses working in this special area.

Stoma care nursing is a microcosm of the challenge inherent in giving good quality nursing care. It is possible to care for the patient with a stoma in a mechanistic way dealing only with physical requirements. But the psychological and social trauma associated with the dysfunction and disfigurement which accompanies a stoma at any site calls for a holist and individualised approach to meeting patients' needs. Only if an assessment of individual physical and psychosocial needs is made, and the nursing care given is designed to meet those needs and carried out with the utmost sensitivity, can it approach to any degree of excellence. Many problems in stoma care present themselves and call for a range of nursing skills – the ability to evaluate and adjust the physical care given, the ability to give reassurance in the initial traumatic stages, the ability to teach the patient and his relatives.

Plainly nurses need education and help in meeting the demands on professional competence in this area. Brigid Breckman has succeeded in gathering together an excellent team of authors who have dealt authoritatively with stoma care nursing. The scientific facts underlying normal functioning form a basis for what follows in the reasons for stomas and their siting. Thereafter there is a wealth of detail on physical and psychosocial aspects of care.

This is a book for nurses written by nurses. The scientific basis for nursing action is accompanied by excellent accounts of different aspects of patient management. These are all given by nurses whose major field of practice has been in stoma care nursing. The result is a truly professional work based firmly in clinical practice which will be useful to students and practitioners alike. Its breadth of treatment must only serve to enhance the approach to nursing care of those who read it. One hopes that it will be followed by other authoritative works on special areas of clinical nursing practice and written by the practitioners themselves.

McFarlane of Llandaff

Preface

Over the past few years nurses in clinical, educational and managerial fields of nursing have frequently asked me three main questions:

1) What is normal stoma care? What should every stoma patient be taught before he goes home? What general overall knowledge should the hospital or community nurse be taught in order that she may promote good stoma care?
2) How may problems in stoma care be identified?
3) How may these problems be solved?

This book has been written in answer to those questions. Chapters 2 to 14 portray the normal pattern of information and care with which health care workers can aid their patients' rehabilitation. Chapters 15 to 17 identify problems which may arise, and suggest solutions. The photographs showing actual and potential siting problems have therefore been placed within this section of the book, although consideration of stoma siting is a normal part of care. Finally, both caregivers and patients are *people* with individual attitudes and needs, the consideration of which is an essential component of stoma care. This is discussed in Chapters 1 and 18.

Throughout the book the patient is almost always referred to as male, and nurses as female. This is to make it clearer whether patients or nurses are being referred to. It is not intended to imply that many more males have stomas than females, or that our male colleagues are any less able or committed to good stoma care than female nurses.

Individual people require individual treatment, and the reader is asked to note, in the rare instances where medication dosages are indicated, that these should not be assumed to be correct for every person. Medical advice and prescription for each individual should always be sought. Trade names are indicated by the use of a capital letter, whereas generic names commence with a small letter.

One area which many nurses find difficult is that of matching the abdominal contours of an individual patient with an appliance which will be suitable for him. Styles of appliances which may be particularly helpful in certain situations are discussed in the text. The line illustrations of appliances have been deliberately simplified, so that useful aspects of their design may be more easily identified.

It is impossible to acknowledge all the people who have provided advice, information and thought-provoking comments as this book progressed to its present form. However special thanks for such help are due to: Di Langelaan, Tutor, Rcn Institute of Advanced Nursing Education; Lyn Marks and Val Speechley, Intravenous Therapy Team, Royal Marsden Hospital; Prilli Stevens, Stomatherapist, Groote Schuur Hospital; Jan Viret, Stoma Care Nurse, Royal Marsden Hospital; Ben Viret, Children's Doctor, Mayday Hospital; and Pat Young, Editor, *Geriatric Medicine*.

Thanks are also due to Reginald R. Hall and Peter D. Ramsden, Consultant Urologists, Freeman Hospital, Newcastle-upon-Tyne, for their advice on Chapter 8; to Christine Clark, Staff Pharmacist, Hope Hospital, Salford, for her detailed comments on the pharmacological content of Chapter 13; to Brenda Marshall, for her meticulous sub-editing; and to the Photographic Departments of the Royal Marsden Hospital and Colchester District Hospitals, for some of the photographs.

Particular thanks are due to Rob Thornton, whose illustrations show such skill and attention to detail.

Finally, on behalf of all the authors, thanks must go to those who consistently displayed faith, patience and support in our endeavours: John Churchill, our publisher; and our husbands, to whom this book is dedicated.

Brigid Breckman

Contents

Chapter 1

Psychosocial Areas Related to Stoma Care

Patients are people. They come from various social, cultural and religious backgrounds, and have been conditioned since childhood to accept certain beliefs, ways of living, and attitudes, producing a unique blend in each individual. In this chapter some of the social and psychological areas which may be important to stoma patients are discussed. Awareness of these areas will help nurses and others involved in the rehabilitation of stoma patients to give the best possible support to each patient, through acceptance of both his individuality and his background. This is not easy, particularly if the nurse is unable to recognise that her own system of beliefs differs from that of the patient, or lacks knowledge of his lifestyle and culture.

THE PATIENT'S BACKGROUND

Knowledge of the cultural and religious background of the patient and his family is most important. Open discussion of intimate matters, such as elimination of urine or faeces, or impairment of sexual function, may not be acceptable in some families. Patients in social classes IV and V may be less able to ask for information, or question medical or nursing treatment, than patients in social classes I and II. Awareness of such difficulties can encourage nurses and doctors to give information and treatment in ways appropriate to the individual concerned.

Various problems can arise for the Muslim patient who requires stoma surgery. Attendance at the five daily prayer meetings involves ritual purification of the body before each meeting. Any discharge from the 'natural openings', i.e. the anus or urethra, is regarded as unclean, and must be cleansed before each prayer meeting. Stomas sited *below* the level of the umbilicus are regarded as 'natural openings' and therefore urine, faeces or flatus passed by them makes the Muslim unclean. A two-piece appliance, or one which can be emptied and flushed out with water, can prevent the Muslim with a stoma from having to change his appliance five times daily, which is likely to cause skin damage.

Stomas sited *above* the umbilicus are not usually regarded as 'natural openings' and thus effluent from them is not regarded as making the Muslim unclean. This fact should be taken into consideration when pre-operative siting of the stoma is carried out. The change in body shape when the Muslim performs the salaam for prayer must also be considered when deciding upon stoma siting.

In some Arab communities any material classed as dirty, such as urine or faeces, must be touched only by the left hand, while the right hand is kept clean for handling food. This can result in Arabs believing that they must use only their left hand for caring for stomas, causing difficulty in application of new bags.

Cleanliness for religious observances and also in the preparation and handling of food plays an important part in the life of Hindus. The presence of a stoma is not always accepted as compatible with the Hindu way of life, and rejection of the ostomist as a suitable marriage partner can also occur.

The Jewish patient may find stoma surgery particularly difficult to accept, because body perfection and freedom from mutilation is expected as part of his religion during life, as well as at the time of death (Speck). Time spent allowing the patient to express his feelings over surgery which is mutilating, and a visit by the Rabbi, where appropriate, can do much to help the patient accept the need for such surgery.

Attitudes towards pain and its acceptance vary considerably in different cultures. The patient from a culture which fosters a stoical attitude towards pain may have difficulty in telling nurses or doctors when he does have pain, even if it is quite severe, or in reporting lack of pain relief from analgesics. Other patients may have no difficulty in expressing fear of pain or indicating its presence (McCaffery). Nurses also have cultural attitudes towards pain and methods of pain relief. It can be difficult for the nurse, whose background has led her to believe that if someone has pain they say so, to recognise when a patient from a culture which does not admit to pain, is in pain, or to assess its severity. Knowledge of different attitudes to pain, how to recognise such attitudes in her patients, and an ability to suggest methods of pain relief which are acceptable to individual patients, are as important in stoma care as in other areas of nursing. The expression of feelings may or may not be acceptable in the patient's culture. In Western countries it is becoming increasingly acceptable for the nurse to encourage the patient to express his feelings. This may be particularly difficult for the man whose culture insists that a stiff upper lip should be maintained at all costs. Acknowledgement of his difficulty, and confirmation that the expression of pain and fear or the shedding of tears is acceptable to the nurse, can be most supportive.

Ostomists, like everyone else, have in time to face death, though not necessarily from the disease which led to their stoma surgery. Cultural attitudes and rituals are of great importance at this time, and the wishes of the patient and his family regarding religious or cultural customs should be respected.

BODY IMAGE

This is the mental picture each individual has of his own body. Body image develops from birth, when the infant is not aware that he is a separate being from his mother. He learns about various parts of the body: how they function and how to gain control over them. Use and mastery of the environment, with evaluation of achievement or failure, will in turn be followed by learning to relate to other people of both sexes. Values and attitudes about acceptability of one's own or other people's bodies will develop through comparison with one's peer group, and thus may be culturally or racially biased. In some parts of the world the slim female figure admired in Western society would be viewed with horror by men who expect women to have generous curves and ample figures. It is commonly acknowledged that surgery resulting in a stoma will also result in a changed body image. It is frequently implied that the only aspect of change for which the patient needs support is the addition of the stoma on the abdominal wall, where it is inevitable that he sees it at appliance changes. Other threats to body image include those involving loss of control at the time of anaesthetic, during surgery, and with the action of the resultant stoma. These will be of varying importance, depending on the individual's adaptation to the environment and normal ways of coping with stress.

Many patients find acceptance of their new form of elimination is easier if it is suggested that the ability to change a bag, at any time and in any place, is a new and acceptable form of control of elimination, which they can adopt as part of their new body image. Others adopt ritualistic and sometimes bizarre methods of coping with elimination. Orbach *et al.* describe special methods used by ostomists to reduce tension during irrigation, such as irrigating between 1–3 a.m. or 4–6 a.m., when interruptions are less likely. Some ostomists viewed their faeces as poisonous, and included in their irrigation routine continual flushing of water over themselves and the toilet to prevent contamination, or the use of substances designed to detoxify the faeces.

Acceptance of the appearance of the stoma may be considerably influenced by people significant in the ostomist's life. It is not uncommon to find a new stoma patient assuming that his partner will be unable to cope with looking at his stoma. Support enabling him to ask his partner if she would like to see an appliance changed (and thus view the stoma), before he leaves hospital, often reveals that the partner is very pleased to accept this invitation. Each couple should be allowed to make their own decision: insistence that the partner must watch an appliance being changed can do more harm than good, as the patient may then not believe that his partner really does accept the stoma. A change of appliance carried out by an informed nurse, willing to answer any questions raised either by the patient or by the partner, can do much to start the patient on the road to acceptance of his new body image. Tactful indication by the nurse that she assumes the patient and his partner will continue their normal sleeping arrangements, and that they will want to know that close contact will not damage the stoma, can open the way for discussion of another potential change in body image for ostomists: altered sexual ability.

Adaptations in body image may well have to be faced by the patient whose sexual ability has been impaired. However, it should not automatically be assumed either that impairment will occur, or that it is at the time of surgery that adaptation to changed ability must take place. The elderly patient, or the patient who has extensive pelvic malignant disease, may have had waning sexual function for some time and have accepted this, as may his partner. The advent of a stoma has also been known to be welcomed as an excellent excuse for avoiding sex by those who dislike or are uninterested in it. It must not be forgotten that ileostomists, with their improved general health following removal of their colon and rectum, may report an improved ability and interest in sex.

Changes in how patients of either sex feel about their sexuality after stoma surgery may be linked with how they perceive their ability to be sexually attractive, or to function sexually, or both. This will partly depend on the view they have had of their desirability and sexual expertise prior to surgery. It will also depend on their perception of the importance attached by their partner to such desirability and expertise, and on how important sexual attractiveness and ability is in their marriage, work and social life.

Support for the ostomist who may have to accept sexual impairment is unfortunately not always regarded as a normal part of care. This is partly due to a dearth of research on the topic, and partly to the attitudes of nurses, doctors and patients towards initiating discussion. Knowledge of the nature and degree of sexual impairment likely to occur with each type of stoma surgery, and whether it will be temporary or permanent, is essential if nurses and doctors are to be able to help patients accept both the physical impairment and the change in body image it can bring. Kolodny *et al.* have made some estimates on male dysfunction, based on discussions with surgeons and ostomists, plus a review of research literature (see Table 1.1). These estimates do not differentiate between physical and psychosocial causes of impairment, or the conditions which necessitated stoma surgery and the extent of surgery carried out. Information on the sexual difficulties of women who have stomas is sparse, with dyspareunia following rectal excision for both ulcerative colitis and cancer being the main complaint which is mentioned.

Table 1.1   Estimated occurrence of disturbed male sexual function after ostomy surgery. From Kolodny, Masters, Johnson and Biggs (1979) *Textbook of Human Sexuality for Nurses*, courtesy Little, Brown & Co.

Type of surgery	Impotence %	Retrograde ejaculation %	Loss of ability to ejaculate %
Ileostomy and removal of rectum	15	5	10
Colostomy and removal of rectum due to cancer	40	50	40
Colostomy and removal of rectum due to other causes	20	30	20
Ileal conduit done in childhood	20	60	30
Ileal conduit done in adulthood	80	20	70

Major changes in body image may take place depending on the disease for which the stoma is raised. The ulcerative colitic patient may view his stoma as a more acceptable means of elimination control, and develop a more positive personality and self-image through loss of his diseased colon and rectum. Improved ability to function socially and at work will enhance his self-image.

The patient who learns he has cancer may have a completely different attitude towards this disease within him and his body image (Breckman). This will vary depending on the individual's concept of cancer and his prognosis – both actual and imagined.

Many people still view cancer as a dirty unsocial disease, and fears that it is contagious or hereditary are sometimes expressed. It is not uncommon for patients, particularly those who have residual or recurrent cancer, to voice fantasies of cancer cells rampaging around their body, sucking its strength like leeches. The patient whose surgery is curative will usually in time accept his new body image as normal, and believe himself to be in charge of his stoma and its care. The patient whose stoma surgery is palliative may find it difficult to perceive his body as anything but one taken over by cancer cells. Stomal action may be classed with vaginal or rectal discharge as visible uncontrollable reminders of the encroaching cancer, and his or her body perceived as undesirable, and unacceptable socially.

The ostomist with Crohn's disease is likely to have to face a changed body image not only at the time of surgery, but also subsequently if the disease recurs and further treatment or surgery is necessary. It can be more difficult for ostomists with Crohn's disease to come to terms with a body image complete with stoma, with the knowledge that stoma surgery is not always curative.

SUPPORT IN ADAPTATION TO ALTERED BODY IMAGE

It is essential for all members of the health care team to accept that the ability to change a bag does not mean that the ostomist has accepted his new body image. Adaptation will depend on what the image change means to the individual patient, its effect on his normal coping mechanisms, the response of family, friends and workmates, and the support available to both patient and family. Adaptation to elective stoma surgery starts pre-operatively. The family's pre-operative behaviour gives a good indication of the support they will offer post-operatively (Dyk and Sutherland). Knowledge of the coping mechanisms used by both patient and family will help nurses in their day-to-day support.

Many ostomists go through a period of mourning for their lost body image. As with bereavement of a friend or member of the family, the phases of numbness, pining and disorganisation, and reorganisation (Bowlby and Parkes) may be experienced over varying periods of time. It can be helpful for the patient and his family to know that this is a normal pattern of behaviour, particularly if they have experienced bereavement in the past, and came to accept their loss eventually.

Pre-operative discussion of what the surgery will mean in terms of changes of lifestyle is most helpful. Removing fears of enormous appliances, odour, social unacceptability, and curtailment of work and social activities, with realistic reassurance over continuation of job, hobbies and the wearing of normal clothes, can help the patient dispense with the unrealistic fears and concentrate on coming to terms with the reality.

Most patients go through a period of regression at the time of their surgery. As they begin to feel they can take responsibility for themselves again, they are likely to try out their acceptability to others by inviting nursing and medical staff to look at their stoma, watching closely for signs of rejection or distaste. Anger and grief may be expressed strongly. If staff cannot accept the patient, and allow him to express and work through these feelings, he may equate rejection of his feelings and behaviour with rejection of himself because of his changed body image. It can be exceedingly difficult to handle an aggressive, demanding, complaining patient who is always critical of his care. Not only will the patient need help to work through this phase, but both his family and the nurses will also need support. The patient who has regressed to taking no responsibility for his own actions or decisions can be equally difficult to handle, particularly for nurses who feel guilty if they do not do everything for the patient.

Support of the patient's normal concept of himself can play a major role in his recovery. The managing director of a major company, accustomed to giving orders and having reports made to him, will find it extra difficult to cope with his surgery if he is constantly told what to do and when, without explanation of why patterns of care are given. If the staff openly acknowledge to the patient their concern that this may be a difficulty for him, it can do much to help both parties to work more harmoniously together to achieve a relaxed, informed patient.

Patients who are expert in a field which is likely to aid them in their stoma care should be encouraged to accept this, without being made to feel the staff expect them to achieve perfect bag changes immediately. The electrician or engineer, used to assessing and matching sizes and shapes of equipment, may feel pride that his expertise in his field will help him to apply a bag more centrally over the stoma. The enthusiastic cook who copes with complicated recipes, and the knitter who enjoys intricate patterns, will feel more capable if they see that this image of capability in themselves is relevant to the new image they are seeking, complete with stoma. It is a part of normal nursing care that assessment of the patient and his concept of self, as it is before surgery, should continue with support after surgery as he seeks, and in most instances finds, acceptance of his new self as a worthy part of his everyday world.

STIGMA

Stigmatisation is an issue that many nurses and doctors are unwilling to discuss with stoma patients. Brusque dismissal of fears that the ostomist may be viewed as less than a normal human being, or cheerful assurances that this will never happen, are neither realistic nor helpful for the patient. An understanding of the concept of stigma, combined with awareness of her own feelings, will enable the nurse to discuss potential problems in this area with the patient as part of his normal rehabilitation programme. Every society has established ways of categorising people, with an accepted list of attributes that are seen as ordinary and natural for members of each of these categories. Social settings establish the categories of people likely to be encountered there. Each person entering a social setting will be categorised by those within it to give him a social identity, which will include personal attributes such as honesty, as well as structural attributes such as occupation. He in turn will categorise the other people within this social setting.

Erving Goffman suggests that people are stigmatised when expectation, based on a value judgement of what their social identity should be, differs from what they actually present to others. When a person's social worth is deemed to be less than anticipated, the result is stigmatisation. An attribute which is seen as stigmatising one individual can be seen as of value in another. Thus it is not the attribute which is the stigma, but only an attribute which is incongruous with the stereotype of what an individual should be. A nurse who learns that a hospital porter has a degree in psychology may view this as inappropriate, and therefore stigmatise him, even though this qualification would enhance the standing of a person in another job. Likewise, the member of the cricket club who learns that the star batsman has an ileostomy may stigmatise him as being of less physical worth, even though he may have just batted a century. The main question which nurses are asked by ostomists and their families is 'Whom do I tell?' Control of information is an area where many patients are ambivalent about their best course of action. Here the nurse can help the patient talk through his own feelings about his stoma: whether he sees it as a stigma; whether he thinks other people will stigmatise him; and finally, how he thinks he will most comfortably handle these situations. Such management must be seen within the context of his acceptance of himself and how he deals with other people's appraisal of him, complete with stoma. Just as the majority of ostomists initially fear that their bag will be visible to everyone they meet, many also fear the stigmatisation that may follow stoma surgery. The nurse who encourages the ostomist and his family to discuss these fears, and how they may best be dealt with, will enable him to view each encounter with his fellow human beings as enjoyable, and not another opportunity to be made to feel different and less than human.

PSYCHOSOCIAL REHABILITATION: WHO DOES WHAT?

Stoma care cannot be separated from the environment within which it is developing. The roles of males and females in society are changing, and so are those of doctors and nurses in the health care team. Acceptance of the need for individualised patient care has brought with it a blurring of the traditional boundaries of areas of care. The designation of which member of the health care team is responsible for each area is less clear-cut. Two hurdles have to be jumped: firstly, what aspects of care should be discussed with the patient, and secondly, whose responsibility is it to discuss them? An increasing amount of research now available indicates areas where the patient and his family may be helped by information. A few examples, cited by Wilson–Barnett in her book on stress in hospital, are indicated here because they are also relevant to stoma care.

Hayward's 1975 study showed that patients who were given comprehensive pre-operative information required fewer analgesics over a defined post-operative period than others. Patients who were more anxious reported more pain, and women required more analgesics than men. It is interesting to note that it was the nurses who determined the amount of analgesia the patients received, how often, and for how long a post-operative period, rather than the patients or doctors.

Boore's 1976 study of patients scheduled for cholecystectomy showed that informed patients had fewer infections post-operatively, and had a significantly lower level of urinary catecholamines and other physiological and psychological indices of stress. Studies by Andrew in 1967 showed that, in a controlled trial, patients previously given information had a reduced anxiety level but could not recall the information. All these studies indicate that information given to the patient will reduce anxiety and stress, resulting in a more relaxed patient who requires less analgesia. None of these studies indicates that the information should be given to patients by designated members of the health care team, but only that it should be given.

Areas where the patient and his family may best be helped by information and counselling are surrounded by emotive responses from all concerned, either in giving or in receiving the care. Perception of the depth of knowledge required in themselves or by their patients will vary enormously between members of the health care team. The main areas of concern in stoma care include:

1) The patient's disease: its extent, availability of treatment to remove or curtail it, and prognosis;
2) Physical and psychological impairment resulting from the disease, from the stoma surgery, and from the patient's perception of what is happening to him;
3) Pain control;
4) Terminal care.

While information on these topics is readily available to all members of the health care team, it is traditionally the surgeon who has assumed responsibility for giving information to the patient, with the medical social worker providing information and counselling where appropriate. With the advent of individualised nursing care and the Nursing Process, many nurses are now discussing these topics with those patients who have identified them as the care-giver with whom they can most easily communicate. As a member of the health care team, the nurse has a responsibility not only to make sure any information she gives to the patient is accurate and appropriate, but also to ensure that other team members are aware of information she has gained. This is particularly important in the field of stoma care, where a number of disciplines will be working together to achieve maximum rehabilitation with the patient.

COUNSELLING

This is an enabling process which is neither teaching, informing nor advising. The definition which is most applicable to stoma care is that given by the Steering Committee of the Standing Committee for the Advancement of Counselling (13) in 1969:

> Counselling is a process through which one person helps another by purposeful conversation in an understanding atmosphere. It seeks to establish a helping relationship in which the one counselled can express his thoughts and feelings in such a way as to clarify his own situation, come to terms with some new experience, see his difficulty more objectively, and so face his problem with less anxiety and tension. Its basic purpose is to assist the individual to make his own decision from among the choices available to him.

The method the counsellor uses to work with her client will usually include:
1) Observation of the client's attitude, including his tone of voice, phraseology, facial expression and way of sitting;
2) Careful listening to what the client says and what he omits to say;
3) Reflection back to the client of what the counsellor thinks he has said, perhaps with observations on feelings he seems to have expressed;
4) Checking with the client whether the counsellor's paraphrasing fits with what the client thinks he has said or felt, and altering her perceptions accordingly.

The fact that the counsellor can hear and accept expressions of feelings, without assigning guilt or innocence, enables the client to start hearing and owning his own feelings, and from there to take the first tentative steps of change.

It is one thing to believe one's patients have a need to be counselled and another to have either the wish or ability to counsel them oneself. Carl Rogers lists some questions he asks himself, and which a would-be counsellor might find helpful:
1) Can I 'be' in some way which will be perceived by the other person as trustworthy, as dependable or consistent in some deep sense?
2) Can I be expressive enough as a person that what I am will be communicated unambiguously?
3) Can I let myself experience positive attitudes toward this other person – attitudes of warmth, caring, liking, interest, respect?
4) Can I be strong enough as a person to be separate from the other?

Can I be a sturdy respecter of my own feelings, my own needs, as well as his?

5) Am I secure enough within myself to permit his separateness? Can I permit him to be what he is – honest or deceitful, infantile or adult, despairing or over-confident? Can I give him the freedom to be?

6) Can I let myself enter fully into the world of his feelings and personal meanings and see these as he does?

7) Can I receive him as he is? Can I communicate this attitude?

8) Can I act with sufficient sensitivity in the relationship that my behaviour will not be perceived as a threat?

9) Can I free him from the threat of external evaluation?

10) Can I meet this other individual as a person who is in process of becoming, or will I be bound by his past and by my past?

Non-directive counselling and acceptance of the patient as a worthwhile individual will do much to help the patient who is anxious about his new body image, and who fears he will be rejected by anyone who knows he has a stoma. Fears of cancer, pain and dying can also be worked through with a counsellor whose concern is to let the patient come to terms with himself and his situation, without imposing her values and attitudes upon him.

Both patient and care-giver will have learnt from childhood to function in certain ways in certain situations, and may do so even though others may see this way of functioning as inappropriate. It is helpful if the nurse is aware of her own methods of coping and of her own defence mechanisms, as well as learning to recognise those of her patients.

This chapter provides few answers for the reader who wants a set of rules with which to rehabilitate stoma patients. Each ostomist is an individual concerned with his own fears and feelings. Awareness of the social and psychological areas discussed in this chapter should encourage nurses and others working with ostomists to help each patient to identify his own areas of concern, and to find acceptable ways of resolving or coming to terms with his individual problems.

SUGGESTED READING

SOCIAL AND CULTURAL CONSIDERATIONS

Breckman, Brigid 1978. The nurse's dilemma in the care of stoma patients. *Rcn. Nursing Standard* April. (Reprints from Coloplast Ltd.)

Kjervik, Diane K. and Martinson, Ida M. 1979. *Women in Stress: a Nursing Perspective.* Appleton–Century–Crofts.

Speck, Peter 1978. *Loss and Grief in Medicine.* Baillière Tindall.

PAIN

McCaffery, Margo 1972. *Nursing Management of the Patient with Pain.* Lippincott.

DYING AND BEREAVEMENT

Kübler, Ross E. 1970. *On Death and Dying.* Tavistock.

Parkes, Colin Murray 1975. *Bereavement.* Penguin.

BODY IMAGE

Norris, Catherine M. 1978. Body image: its relevance to professional nursing. In *Behavioural Concepts and Nursing Intervention,* Carlson and Blackwell (eds). Lippincott.

SEX

Comfort, Alex 1975. *The Joy of Sex.* Quartet.

Kolodny, Robert C., Masters, William H., Johnson, Virginia E. and Biggs, Mae A. 1980. *Textbook of Human Sexuality for Nurses.* Little, Brown.

Heslinga, K. 1974. *Not Made of Stone. The Sexual Problems of Handicapped People.* Charles C. Thomas, U.S.A. or Noordhoff International Publishing, Leyden, The Netherlands.

STIGMA

Blackwell, Betty 1978. Stigma. In *Behavioural Concepts and Nursing Intervention.* Carlson and Blackwell (eds). Lippincott.

Goffman, Erving 1968. *Stigma. Notes on the Management of Spoiled Identity.* Penguin.

COMMUNICATION AND COUNSELLING

Balint M. 1968. *The Doctor, his Patient and the Illness.* Pitman.
Balint, E. and Norrell, J. S. 1973. *Six Minutes for the Patient.* Tavistock.
Berne, Eric 1968. *Games People Play.* Penguin.
Burton, Genevieve 1980. *Interpersonal Relations. A Guide for Nurses* 4th edition. Tavistock.
Nurse, Gaynor 1980. *Counselling and the Nurse.* H.M. and M.
Rogers, C. R. 1965. *Client-centred Therapy.* Constable.
Rogers, C. R. 1961. *On Becoming a Person.* Constable.
Steiner, Claud 1975. *Scripts People Live.* Bantam.

REFERENCES

*Andrew, J. M. 1967. Coping Styles. Stress-relevant learning and recovery from surgery. PhD dissertation, Los Angeles, University of California.
*Boore, J. R. P. 1976. An investigation into the effects of some aspects of pre-operative preparation of patients on post-operative stress and recovery. PhD thesis, University of Manchester.
Bowlby, J. and Parkes, C. M. 1970. Separation and Loss. In *The Child in his Family. International Yearbook of Child Psychiatry and Allied Professions 1,* ed. Anthony, E. J. and Koupernik, C. Wiley.
Breckman, Brigid 1979. Care of the Stoma Patient. *Proceedings of the Nursing Mirror International Cancer Nursing Conference,* 1978.
Dyk, R. B. and Sutherland, A. M. 1956. Adaptation of the spouse and other family members to the colostomy patient. *Cancer 9,* 123–38.
Goffman, Erving 1968. *Stigma. Notes on the Management of Spoiled Identity.* Penguin.
*Hayward, J. 1975. *Information – a Prescription against Pain.* London. Rcn Study of Nursing Care.
Kolodny, R. C. *et al.* 1979. *Textbook of Human Sexuality for Nurses.* Little, Brown.
McCaffery, Margo 1972. *Nursing Management of the Patient with Pain,* 44–52. Lippincott.
Orbach *et al.* 1957. Fears and defensive adaptations to the loss of anal sphincter control. *Psychoanalytic Review 44,* 121–75.
Rogers, Carl R. 1967. *On Becoming a Person,* 50–51. Constable.
Speck, Peter 1978. *Loss and Grief in Medicine.* Baillière Tindall.
Steering Committee of the Standing Committee for the Advancement of Counselling 1969. In *Counselling and the Nurse* 2nd edition, 1980, p. 2. Gaynor Nurse. H.M. and M.

* (*See* Wilson-Barnett, J. 1979. *Stress in Hospital,* 58–9. Churchill Livingstone.)

QUESTIONS FOR DISCUSSION

1) What factors should be taken into consideration when siting a stoma pre-operatively for a Muslim patient?
2) What is body image?
3) List four ways in which an ostomist may feel his body image has altered because of his surgery.
4) Give three ways in which the nurse may support the stoma patient as he adapts to his new body image.
5) How may the nurse help her patients to decide whom they should tell about their stoma?
6) What is counselling?
7) Give four ways in which a counsellor may work with her client.

Chapter 2

The Normal Function of the Alimentary Tract

Digestion exists for health, and health exists for life, and life exists for the love of music or beautiful things.

G. K. Chesterton

Whatever one's views on the purpose of life, it is an indisputable fact that our digestive ability is a major determinant of our health. Whether, by circumstances or geography, we are condemned to a diet of rice or maize, or gorge ourselves on duck à l'orange and pâté, it is a fact that the food we eat, whatever its nature, is rapidly converted by our bodies to just a few basic chemicals and thus we become what we eat. It is with this process that this chapter is concerned.

The adult human gastrointestinal tract consists of a tube of variable diameter, some 4.5m (15ft) in length from mouth to anus, the function of which is to make ingested food substances easily diffusable, so that they may be absorbed and assimilated (see Figure 2.1).

Throughout the length of the tract, proteins are broken down into amino acids, carbohydrates into monosaccharides and fats into fatty acids and glycerol. These latter substances are of such a size and form that they can pass through the gut wall, thus being made available to the body for metabolism and assimilation, together with vitamins, minerals and water. The volume of digestive juices secreted daily is shown in Table 2.1 (page 20).

In order to carry out this work, the structure of the tube is intimately fitted to its function, and the two aspects should always be looked at together. When considering what a portion of the gut *does*, one should ask what design features are built into this area of the gut to allow it to carry out this function.

A few general rules can be stated here:

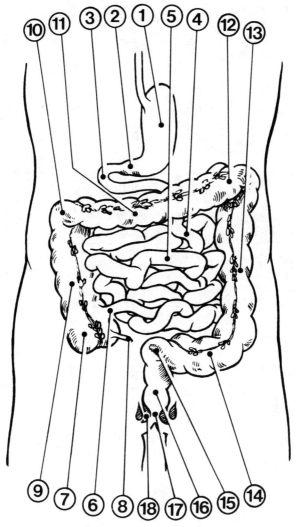

Figure 2.1   The gastrointestinal tract (see Key, following).

1) Where food is initially taken into the body, there has to be a means of breaking it into smaller pieces.
Hence: teeth – incisors for tearing, molars for grinding.

Figure 2.1 KEY TO DIAGRAM OF GASTROINTESTINAL TRACT

Anatomical area	Approximate time required for food substances to reach this area	Consistency	Function
1. STOMACH	1–5 mins depending on diet	Depends on intake Usually fairly coarse	Storage of food. Mixing with gastric secretions to form chyme. Protein digestion started. Absorption of alcohol.
2. PYLORIC SPHINCTER			Allows chyme to empty into duodenum at a suitable rate for digestion.
3. DUODENUM			Movements allow mixing with pancreatic juice and bile. Absorption of calcium, magnesium and iron. Partial digestion of proteins, fats and starch.
4. JEJUNUM		Fluid and bile-stained	Mixing with intestinal juices here and ileum allows further digestion of proteins, fats and carbohydrates.
5. ILEUM		In some patients may, at times, be the consistency of toothpaste	Absorption in proximal portion of fat-soluble and water-soluble vitamins, monosaccharides and disaccharides. Absorption in terminal portion of sodium, potassium, chloride, bicarbonate, vitamin B_{12} and bile salts. Water is absorbed in both.
6. ILEO-CAECAL VALVE	4–5 hours		Controls passage of residue into large intestine.
7. CAECUM		Fluid — slightly creamy	Receives chyme from small intestine. Absorbs water.

Structure	Time	Consistency / Stool	Function
8. APPENDIX			Contains lymph nodules
9. ASCENDING COLON		Becoming thicker (like thin porridge)	Absorption of: Water (mainly in ascending colon) Sodium, potassium, chloride Glucose Rectally administered drugs
10. RIGHT COLIC (HEPATIC) FLEXURE	6–7 hours		
11. TRANSVERSE COLON		Stiffer consistency (like very thick porridge)	Secretes mucus to lubricate faeces
12. LEFT COLIC (SPLENIC) FLEXURE	9–10 hours		Intestinal bacteria synthesise vitamin K
13. DESCENDING COLON			
14. PELVIC (SIGMOID) COLON		Firm, solid separate stools	
15. PELVIC (SIGMOID) FLEXURE	12–24 hours		
16. RECTUM	Varies in individuals Can take 4–5 days	Stool appearance will depend on diet. If bran intake is adequate, the stool passed will be semi-solid and form a pancake like the cow's.	Storage of faeces
17. ANAL CANAL			
18. INTERNAL AND EXTERNAL ANAL SPHINCTERS			Controls passage of faeces to exterior. Only external sphincter under voluntary control.

2) Food substances are to be broken down chemically as well as mechanically, so they have to be partially liquefied and well-mixed.

Hence: sac-like form of stomach and its internal muscle arrangement, which allows churning and conversion of food into minestrone soup-like consistency.

3) Enzymes must be secreted into this mixture to bring about breakdown as required.

Hence: areas of digestion are highly vascular, vasodilation occurring during periods of activity. Large surface area provided. Muscle arrangement allows for further mixing with digestive juices.

4) There has to be a means of moving substances along this 4.5m of tube.

Hence: muscle arrangement in walls of gut which allows movement as necessary; secretion of mucus where movement is slow.

5) Having broken down food substances, the gut must absorb the resulting products along with water; digestive juices too must be reabsorbed.

Hence: large surface area for absorption – villi and brush borders to cells.

6) The non-absorbable substances and debris must be eliminated from the body.

Hence: structure allows for storage of debris so that the need for elimination is not constant – sphincters allow elimination at convenient intervals.

Table 2.1   Daily secretion of digestive juices

Secretion	Volume	pH
Saliva	1000–1500ml	6.0–7.0
Gastric juice	2000ml	1.5–3.5
Pancreatic juice	1500–2000ml	7.8–8.0
Bile	500–1000ml	7.8–8.0
Intestinal juice	3000ml	7.8–8.0

This chapter is principally concerned with the normal function of the small and large bowel and the rectum. However, it will be necessary to consider what has gone on in the gut before the food gets to the small intestine, in order to understand the work of the latter.

THE MOUTH

The mouth is a cavity equipped with incisor teeth to tear food into pieces, and muscular lips both to guard the entrance and to help to pull food into the cavity. Once solid food is in the mouth, it is ground up into smaller pieces by the molars and premolars. The jaws can move both horizontally and vertically, allowing the food, formed into a bolus by the teeth and mixed with saliva, to be moved around the cavity and mechanically pounded.

Saliva is secreted by the three pairs of salivary glands:
1) Parotid;
2) Submandibular;
3) Sublingual.

Saliva has a pH of about 6.8, although at times it may be slightly alkaline. 1000 to 1500ml are secreted each day. It is made up largely of water (99 per cent) containing sodium and potassium chloride, sodium bicarbonate, calcium carbonate, sodium phosphate and calcium phosphate. As far as digestion is concerned, its most important constituent is salivary amylase: this acts on cooked starch and converts it to dextrins and maltose. This enzyme acts until the gastric acid inactivates it. It may thus continue to work for about 20 minutes. Mucin is a further constituent of saliva which helps to bind the food substances together.

Apart from its digestive function, saliva is necessary for:
1) Speech;
2) Moistening and cleaning the mouth (it is slightly bactericidal);
3) Appreciation of taste. The taste buds on the tongue are only stimulated by chemicals in solution;
4) Swallowing.

Saliva is secreted in response to autonomic stimulation. The sympathetic nerves bring about a scanty secretion which is rich in enzymes; the parasympathetic system stimulates a copious discharge rich in salts. Secretion is brought about by:
1) Mechanical stimulation – presence of food in the mouth;
2) The sight, thought or smell of food: this is a conditioned reflex.

SWALLOWING

This is the act which propels the bolus from the foyer to the tract proper. It is vital that the food does not go either into the lungs or into the nasal cavity, and thus safeguards are built into the act to prevent uneconomical and indeed dangerous misdirection. The bolus is gathered onto the upper surface of the tongue and pressed against the hard palate and backwards towards the pharynx. In order to prevent the food going upwards in the pharynx and into the nasal cavities, the soft palate rises and thus shuts off this route. Swallowing receptors in the area of the tonsils and the pharynx are stimulated, and impulses are sent to the medulla, which triggers off the swallowing reflex. The larynx rises upwards, with its vocal chords drawn together, closing the glottis. The epiglottis turns backwards. These actions prevent food from entering the respiratory tract.

The bolus is now able to enter the oesophagus. A wave of peristalsis carries the bolus rapidly into the upper part of the tube, frequently with a small amount of air that is usually later expelled by belching. Once in the oesophagus, ring-like waves of contraction grip the bolus and transfer it to the cardiac (gastro-oesophageal) sphincter of the stomach. The peristaltic wave allows the sphincter to relax, and the bolus thus enters the stomach. The length of time taken for this will depend on the size and consistency of the bolus: for example, liquids will take only one to two seconds to travel the 25cm of the oesophagus and arrive at the stomach.

The first stage of swallowing is under voluntary control and can be halted at will. Once the bolus reaches the pharynx, however, the act becomes inevitable and purely reflex, and respiration is inhibited.

THE GASTROINTESTINAL TRACT

STRUCTURE OF THE WALL OF THE GASTROINTESTINAL TRACT

The general structure of the tube along which the food is to be propelled can now be considered. It consists of four main layers which are basically similar throughout the tract. There are alterations from the general pattern where areas of the gut perform distinctly different functions (e.g. stomach and colon).

1) *Mucosa*

This is the innermost layer (i.e. it is nearest the lumen) and is made up of epithelial cells and the secretory glands. It is well supplied with small blood and lymphatic vessels, and has a very thin layer of muscle called the *muscularis mucosae*. The mucosa is secretory and absorptive, and the thin muscle layer allows the surface area to be expanded as necessary. The lymph vessels are protective; lymph follicles are commonly present along the length of the small and large intestine in both the mucosa and submucosa.

2) *Submucosa*
This layer is made up of dense connective tissue which binds the surface mucosa to the deeper muscle layer. The blood vessels and lymphatics contained here are larger. A network of nerve endings is present here, called the *submucosal plexus (Meissner's plexus)*.

3) *Muscular*
The muscle layer consists of smooth muscle throughout the whole of the tract, except in the pharynx and upper one-third of the oesophagus where striated muscle is present. Usually (except in the stomach) the muscle fibres are arranged in two sheets: a circular inner sheet of fibres and a longitudinal outer sheet. In the colon this longitudinal sheet is incomplete. Between the two sheets of fibres, there is a network of neurones called the *myenteric plexus (Auerbach's plexus)*.

This muscle layer is responsible for the wave-like movements of the gut wall, and hence the transport of food substances through the tube. Localised contractions allow mixing of the substances and alteration of the diameter of the lumen.

4) *Serous*
This layer is present only where there is mesentery surrounding or suspending the gut. It consists of a layer of peritoneal tissue which carries blood, lymph vessels and nerves to the gut. Where this is absent, there is a layer of adventitia or connective tissue.

REGULATION OF THE GASTROINTESTINAL SYSTEM

Regulation of secretion and movement throughout the gut is both hormonal (humoral) and nervous. Hormonal control will be dealt with later when the intestine is described in detail.

Nervous control is via the autonomic nervous system. Sympathetic and parasympathetic nerve fibres enter the gastrointestinal tract, and synapse with neurones in the submucosal and myenteric plexuses. These plexuses form the local internal nervous system of the gut. Autonomic fibres in addition have direct connections with glands and smooth muscle in the tract.

The internal nerve plexuses are present throughout the length of the tube from oesophagus to rectum, and consist of a network of neurones supplying the glands and smooth muscle fibres. Neurones of one plexus synapse with those of the other, and hence their effects are inter-related. Their arrangement allows stimulation at the upper end of the tract to cause excitation at a distance. This explains why secretion is evident in glands in the small intestine upon swallowing of food.

The vagus is the major autonomic nerve supplying the gut. It has branches to the stomach, small intestine and upper portion of the large intestine. It is a mixed nerve, and thus carries efferent fibres from the parasympathetic system to the gut wall and afferent fibres from gut wall receptors to the brain. The distal colon receives its parasympathetic supply from the *nervi erigentes*. Parasympathetic stimulation gives rise to a generalised increase in activity of the internal plexuses and excitation of the gut. Sympathetic innervation originates from the spinal cord between T.8 and L.3 and travels via the sympathetic chain of ganglia. The sympathetic opposes the parasympathetic system in general, and causes slowing and inhibition of gastrointestinal tract activity.

To summarise autonomic control:

Organ	Parasympathetic stimulation	Sympathetic stimulation
Stomach	Increased motility Relaxes sphincters Increases secretion	Decreased motility Contracts sphincters Inhibits secretion
Intestine	Increased motility Relaxes sphincters Increases secretion	Decreased motility Contracts sphincters

MOVEMENTS OF THE INTESTINES

Bayliss and Starling were the first physiologists to describe the main gut movement, peristalsis, in 1899. The movement consists of a double action: contraction above the section and relaxation below, which ensures that food substances are squeezed along the tube. Peristalsis moves down the intestine in one direction. It depends on the myenteric reflex triggered off in the internal plexus, and can be excited by parasympathetic stimuli.

Other movements of the gut appear to be adaptations of this basic mechanism. Pendular movements consist of gentle waves of contraction initiating rhythmic lengthening and shortening of portions of the intestine. Segmentation and mass movement are described in relation to the colon.

THE STOMACH

The stomach is a sac-like dilatation of the tube described above. It is frequently described as J-shaped, although it exhibits considerable variation in shape and position from person to person. When empty, the stomach is almost tube-like, having a volume of only about 50ml. It can distend after a meal, and when full holds nearly 1000ml.

The surface of the stomach is folded into rugae, which allow distension to take place and enlarge the surface area for secretion and absorption of some water, about 20 per cent of alcohol and some drugs, e.g. aspirin.

The stomach acts as a reservoir for food and can regulate the rate at which its contents are propelled into the small intestine. The importance of this function is evident after a total gastrectomy, when the food is sometimes propelled so rapidly into the small intestine that digestion and absorption are inadequate.

Food normally begins to leave the stomach less than 30 minutes after it is eaten, although there will be considerable variation depending on the consistency and composition of the meal. Emptying, however, is usually complete after 4–5 hours, although this time may be shortened by emotional states, such as fear, and increased by the action of some drugs, e.g. anticholinergics and some antidepressants.

The pressure within the stomach is +5 to +10mm Hg, i.e. above· atmospheric pressure, due to the pressure exerted on it by the abdominal contents. The presence of the cardiac sphincter is thus important to prevent reflux of food into the oesophagus.

The structure of the stomach wall differs from that of the tube previously described, in that the muscular coat has three layers instead of two. Longitudinal (outermost), circular and oblique (innermost) fibres are present which facilitate the unique churning movements of the stomach. These movements convert the food intake into chyme – a thick, soup-like solution of food, water and enzymes.

The longitudinal and circular layers are continuous with the oesophagus, and form the pyloric sphincter at the distal end of the stomach which mechanically prevents untimely emptying.

There are three types of cells present in the secretory epithelium of the stomach:

1) *Mucous cells*

These are present in the pylorus and secrete mucus, which is also produced from the necks of the tubular glands elsewhere in the stomach. A layer of mucus one mm thick is necessary to prevent autodigestion of the stomach wall by the protein digesting enzymes produced by the chief cells. The mucus is slightly alkaline.

2) *Chief cells* (peptic cells)

These secrete pepsinogen, the inactive precursor of pepsin. Gastric acid activates the pepsinogen, and the resultant pepsin breaks down protein into proteoses and peptones (polypeptides). Only a small amount (about 10 per cent) of protein is acted upon in the stomach. The remaining 90 per cent of protein digestion takes place in the small intestine.

In infants, rennin is also secreted. It acts upon casein, a soluble protein in milk, converting it to paracasein. This combines with calcium ions to form the curd. This function is taken over by hydrochloric acid in the adult.

3) *Parietal cells* (oxyntic cells)

These cells contain carbonic anhydrase, an enzyme, which facilitates the production of a) hydrochloric acid secreted into the lumen of the stomach and b) bicarbonate secreted into the blood. The acid produced is neutralised somewhat by the gastric mucus and the buffering effect of proteins in the diet. However, the resultant pH of gastric fluid is in the range of 1.5 to 3.5. Hydrochloric acid, in addition to its role in activating pepsinogen, is bactericidal, inactivates salivary amylase and tenderises and denatures (i.e. alters the structure of) fibrous proteins.

The parietal cells also secrete intrinsic factor, a protein necessary for the absorption of vitamin B_{12} from the terminal ileum. The secretion from all three types of cells amounts to about 2000ml per day.

SUMMARY OF FUNCTIONS OF THE STOMACH

1) Receives food and acts as reservoir;
2) Controls output of food into the duodenum;
3) Mixes food with gastric juice to form chyme;
4) Produces gastric juice (as shown in Table 2.2). This contains:
    a) pepsinogen, a precursor of pepsin which starts protein digestion,
    b) mucus to protect the stomach lining,
    c) intrinsic factor for absorption of vitamin B_{12},
    d) hydrochloric acid which is bactericidal and which inactivates salivary amylase,
    e) rennin, in infants, to curdle milk;
5) Absorbs some water, alcohol and drugs.

Table 2.2 Gastric juice secretion.

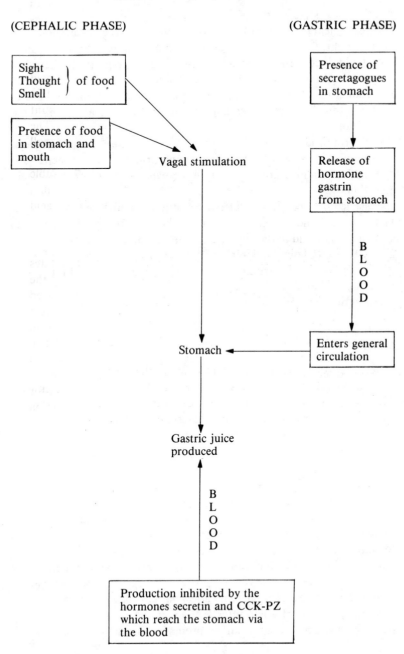

CONTROL OF SECRETION

The flow of gastric juice is stimulated by:
1) Mechanical presence of food in the stomach via the vagus nerve;
2) The sight, thought or smell of food via a conditioned reflex – often called the cephalic or psychic phase of gastric digestion. The vagus nerve is also responsible for this secretion;
3) Production of gastrin, which is a hormone released in response to certain foods called secretagogues – particularly meat, caffeine and alcohol.

The gastrin produced by the stomach is absorbed into the gastric blood vessels, circulates back to the stomach and brings about an increase in hydrochloric acid secretion. This is known as the gastric phase of digestion.

Gastric juice secretion and gastric motility are inhibited by:
1) Secretin, a hormone, produced by the wall of the duodenum in response to acid in the chyme entering it;
2) CCK–PZ (Cholecystokinin–pancreozymin) a hormone produced by the wall of the duodenum in response to amino acids and fatty acids in the food entering it.

These actions prevent sudden duodenal overloading.

GASTRIC EMPTYING

When gastric digestion is completed, peristaltic waves starting in the antrum propel small amounts of chyme through the pylorus into the duodenum. When the duodenum is full, it sends impulses via the vagus and the myenteric plexus to slow gastric emptying, until its contents have passed on and it is free to receive more chyme from the stomach.

THE SMALL INTESTINE

This is a long, coiled tube about 2.5m (9ft) long in the living body, somewhat longer in death due to relaxation. The function of this tube is to complete the digestion of food and to absorb practically all of the nutrients and most of the water from the chyme. About 50 per cent of this part of the gut can be removed before there is an appreciable effect on digestion and absorption. Only a few patients have survived with less than 25 per cent of their intestine remaining intact. Loss of large portions of the ileum can result in problems with loss of bile salts and vitamin B_{12}, and poor absorption of fat, fat-soluble vitamins and calcium.

The small intestine consists of the C-shaped (wider) duodenum (25cm), the loop of which contains the pancreas, the jejunum (0.9m) and the ileum. These areas are not structurally distinct.

DUODENUM

By the time the chyme reaches the duodenum, not a great deal of digestion has occurred. We have seen that cooked starches have been converted to dextrins and maltose, and 10 per cent of protein has been broken down into polypeptides. The duodenum is a fairly short tube. Its name (derived from the Latin) implies that it is twelve fingers in length, or about 21–25cm long.

The structure of its wall follows the broad pattern described earlier. The duodenum does not itself produce any digestive enzymes, but does however secrete hormones. It receives the secretions of the pancreatic and bile ducts at a point some 10cm below the pylorus of the stomach through a common orifice. Thus the duodenum plays a major role in digestion.

The secretions poured into the duodenum from these two glands (the liver and pancreas) are alkaline. There is therefore a sharp change in the pH of the intestinal contents, from the gastric pH of 1.5 to 3.5 to the duodenal pH (after the addition of bile or pancreatic juice) of 7.8 to 8.0. This latter high pH is necessary since the digestive enzymes of the small intestine are pH-specific and act only in an alkaline medium.

The first part of the duodenum must be protected, like the stomach, from the acid entering it. In the first few centimetres, there are a large number of mucus-secreting glands (Brünner's glands). Some authorities postulate the presence of a hormone, duocrinin, which they say is secreted from the intestinal mucosa and stimulates the production of mucus.

THE PANCREAS

This is shaped like an elongated triangle. Its base or head is embraced by the C-shaped curve of the duodenum, and its tail projects to the left side of the abdomen. It is 12–15cm long, pink in colour and has a somewhat delicate texture when compared to, say, the liver.

It carries out both endocrine (the secretion of insulin and glucagon) and exocrine functions. Only the latter will be discussed here.

In its fine structure, the pancreas resembles a salivary gland, being composed of rather loosely-packed compound glands. The exocrine functions are carried out by cells that are grouped together into units rather like bunches of grapes. These cell units are called *acini* ('acinus' being the Latin for grape). The ducts from the acini coalesce to form the tributaries which enter the main pancreatic duct. It is thought that the bicarbonate content of the pancreatic juice is secreted by cells lining the tubes leading from the acini. The main pancreatic duct runs the length of the gland. Close to the duodenum, this duct joins the common bile duct and both enter the duodenum at the sphincter of Oddi.

Pancreatic juice
There are in effect two separate secretions produced by the pancreas: one rich in sodium bicarbonate and the other rich in enzymes.

1) *Bicarbonate secretion*
Each day, 1500 to 2000ml of bicarbonate-rich secretion, with a pH of 7.8 to 8.0, is poured out of the pancreatic duct into the duodenum. This is an active process, i.e. it uses energy. It is thought to be the reverse of the process described earlier, carried out by the parietal cells of the stomach. The cells of the pancreas contain carbonic anhydrase, and this (it is thought) allows: a) the production of bicarbonates poured into the lumen of the duct, and b) the production of acid, which is secreted into the blood leaving the pancreas. This acid may be neutralised by the bicarbonate in the blood leaving the stomach, as described earlier.

Normally, most of the bicarbonate which is secreted into the gut is reabsorbed, so there is little absolute loss from the body. Thus it can be seen that in diarrhoea, or in any case where there is intestinal hurry or where major absorptive areas of the gut have been surgically removed, bicarbonate may not be reabsorbed adequately and so acidosis is a potential problem.

When food is present in the duodenum, the rate of secretion increases and so does the bicarbonate content.

2) *Enzyme secretion*
Enzymes are produced for each of the three food groups. As in the stomach, enzymes which are designed to digest proteins must be secreted in an inactive precursor form, in order to prevent autodigestion of the intestinal wall or the secreting organ (see Table 2.3).
a) *Trypsin*. For the reasons stated above, this proteolytic enzyme is

Table 2.3   Pancreatic juice secretion.

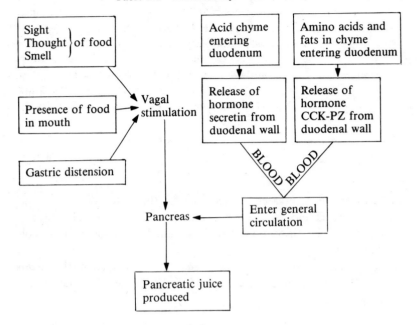

secreted as the inactive trypsinogen. A co-enzyme, enterokinase, is secreted by the duodenal mucosa, and this breaks a bond between two amino acids in the trypsinogen molecule to form active trypsin. Calcium can also carry out this function. Once trypsin is formed, it can itself activate further trypsinogen and can also activate another proteolytic enzyme produced by the pancreas, chymotrypsinogen, which is converted to chymotrypsin.

Both chymotrypsin and trypsin act on proteins and polypeptides, and convert them to peptides (smaller sections of amino acids) as shown in Table 2.4. There is a further proteolytic enzyme present in pancreatic juice called carboxypeptidase. This acts on some peptides to split off their terminal amino acid.

b) *Amylase*. This is more active than the salivary amylase discussed earlier. It acts on polysaccharides and splits them into maltose and dextrins. Some glucose may also be produced at this stage. Pancreatic diastase also helps in converting starch to maltose.

c) *Lipase*. The pancreatic juice contains the main lipolytic enzyme produced by the gut. It splits fats into highly insoluble fatty acids and glycerol. Before lipase can act, emulsification of fats is necessary in

Table 2.4   Action of chymotrypsin and trypsinogen.

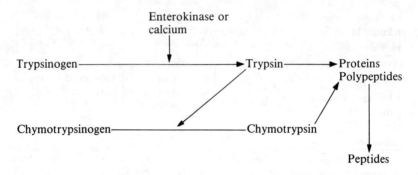

order to provide a greater surface area for the action of the enzyme. This is carried out by the bile salts (see below), which are also necessary for the absorption of the resultant fatty acids made soluble by these salts.

d) *Ribonuclease and deoxyribonuclease.* These act on nucleic acids (DNA, RNA) present in ingested food, and split them into nucleotides for resynthesis.

Control of pancreatic secretion

1) *Nervous*
This is via the vagus nerve, which is parasympathetic and thus excitatory. In addition to having a direct effect, the vagus increases the reaction of the acinar cells (the exocrine pancreatic cells) to the duodenal hormones. Vagal stimulation may result from the sight, thought or smell of food, or the presence of food in the mouth. Gastric distension, too, results (via the vagus) in pancreatic secretion. The secretion thus produced is rich in enzymes.

2) *Hormonal*
There are two main hormones produced by the duodenal mucosa. Both, when secreted, enter the circulation and travel round the body to the pancreas to bring about pancreatic secretion.

a) *Secretin.* This was the first hormone to be discovered, by Bayliss and Starling in 1902. Its secretion is brought about by acid chyme entering the duodenum. It acts mainly on the ducts leading from the acini in the pancreas, and thus its function is to elicit a copious secretion rich in bicarbonate. The hormone is in itself a peptide, consisting of twenty-seven amino acids.

b) *Cholecystokinin–pancreozymin.* In the 1920s, it was found that when fats entered the duodenum, bile was released from the gall bladder. The hormone which brought this about was named *cholecystokinin.* In the 1940s, it was found that when food entered the duodenum, a hormone was produced that encouraged the production of an enzyme-rich secretion from the pancreas. This hormone was named *pancreozymin.* It has now been found that these two substances are almost identical, and are thus referred to as *cholecystokinin–pancreozymin,* or *CCK–PZ,* or just as *cholecystokinin* or as *CCK.*

Part of the CCK–PZ molecule has a structure similar to gastrin, mentioned earlier. Thus, CCK–PZ stimulates gastric acid secretion. Gastrin, similarly, is quite effective in bringing about pancreatic enzyme secretion, and has a mild effect in causing gall bladder contraction. Secretion of CCK–PZ is in response to the amino acids and fats present in the chyme entering the duodenum. The release of both of the duodenal hormones inhibits gastric secretion and motility, thus giving time for the duodenal contents to be neutralised and digested.

THE LIVER

This has many functions, but only the manufacture of bile will be discussed here (see Table 2.5).

Bile composition
This is a yellow-brown viscous water-based fluid, bitter to the taste, with a pH of about 7.8. It contains:

1) *Bile pigments*
These are principally bilirubin with some biliverdin, formed from the breakdown of haemoglobin released from worn-out red blood cells. The bile pigments are formed in the reticulo-endothelial system, and travel to the liver bound to albumen. In the liver, they are combined chemically, i.e. *conjugated,* with glucuronic acid, made water-soluble and secreted into the bile, where they are responsible for its yellow colour. The bile therefore forms an excretory transport route for these waste products.

As they pass through the gut, the pigments are altered by the digestive enzymes and bacterial action, and are converted into stercobilinogen and then stercobilin. These give the brown colouration to the faeces.

Some of the pigments are reabsorbed into the portal blood vessels during their passage through the gut. Of these, some will recirculate to the liver for re-excretion, and the rest will be excreted in the urine as urobilinogen, which helps to give the urine its yellow colour.

2) *Bile salts*

As far as digestion is concerned, these are the most important constituents of bile. Normally, these salts are recycled, only about 20 per cent being lost from the body. During a meal, four to eight grams of bile salts may be secreted into the duodenum, of which 80 per cent will be reabsorbed in the ileum.

In the liver, cholic acid – a derivative of cholesterol – is conjugated with the amino acids taurine and glycine to form the bile salts taurocholic acid and glycocholic acid. These salts act as detergents, lowering the surface tension of the large globules of fat in the chyme which enter the duodenum. The globules are broken down into fine droplets about one nanometer across. These droplets are called micelles and can take up fat-soluble vitamins. The fats thus emulsified can now be acted upon by the pancreatic lipase. Bile salts are also necessary for the efficient absorption of both iron and the fat-soluble vitamins (A, D, E and K).

3) *Cholesterol*

This, chemically, is a sterol and is thus related to the sex hormones, vitamin D and the adrenal steroids in that it has a similar molecular structure. The bile salts and another phospholipid substance present in the bile called lecithin make cholesterol water-soluble, so that the watery bile can act as its medium of excretion.

Normally, this excretion is trouble-free, but if there are large amounts of cholesterol to be excreted, as might be found with a diet consistently rich in animal fats, or if the levels of bile salts or lecithin are low, the cholesterol may precipitate out of solution and gallstones may be formed.

4) Bile also contains the protein mucin, fatty acids and the usual electrolytes found in plasma.

Bile secretion

As the chyme enters the duodenum it provides the stimulus for the

Table 2.5 Formation and secretion of bile.

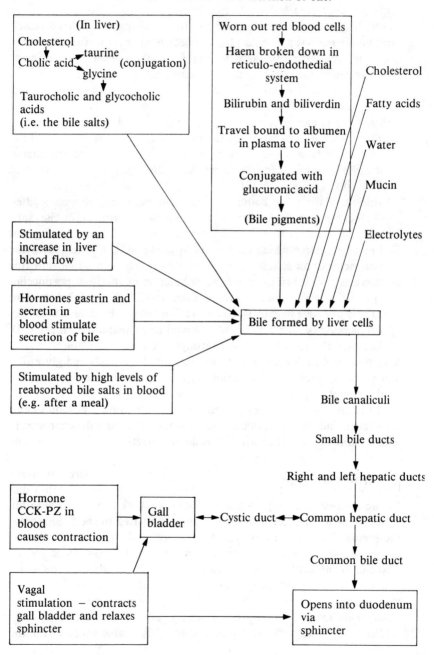

release of bile and its secretion into the duodenum. Between 500 and 1000ml are secreted daily.

Bile is secreted by the liver cells into the small canaliculi that radiate throughout the liver lobules. It is collected up by the terminal bile ducts, finally entering the hepatic duct. It can then either be stored and concentrated in the gall bladder, or poured directly into the duodenum via the common bile duct. It is possible for the gall bladder to concentrate the bile by five to ten times.

Bile secretion is continuous, but can be stimulated by:

1) The presence of bile salts in the blood. After a meal, bile salts are reabsorbed from the gut and enter the blood. High levels stimulate the rate at which liver cells secrete bile salts.

Thus, it can be seen that if the major proportion of bile salts are lost absolutely from the body, as with an ileostomy, then one of the stimuli for bile salt secretion is decreased and production is thus reduced.

2) The vagus nerve which relaxes the sphincter of Oddi, and helps to contract the gall bladder.

3) Secretin which brings about the production of the fluid portion of bile. CCK–PZ helps in this, as does gastrin. CCK–PZ is particularly effective in causing contraction of the gall bladder.

4) An increase in liver blood flow. This will be evident after a meal.

So, when the food has passed through the duodenum, the proteins have been broken down into peptides, fats into fatty acids and glycerol, and carbohydrates to disaccharides (mainly maltose), dextrins and a small amount of glucose.

It remains, therefore, for protein and carbohydrate digestion to be completed, and for absorption to take place. Both these will occur in the jejunum and ileum, which will be considered together.

JEJUNUM AND ILEUM

Before discussing the digestive and absorptive work carried out here, it is necessary to consider how the structure is related to the function of the region. The basic four-layered structure of the gut wall has been discussed earlier. In this region, the mucosa of the basic structure is modified for absorption and secretion.

If the maximum amount of nutrients from the liquid passing down the tube is to be extracted, there must be a large surface area. Furthermore, there must be a good blood supply. Thus the mucosa is highly folded (into the *valvulae conniventes*), and it is further thrown up into about five million finger-like processes called *villi,* each about 1mm in height. In turn, the villi have on their surfaces even smaller projections called *microvilli.* Each cell has about a thousand of these microvilli, forming a 'brush border'. Each villus is supplied with a capillary network and a small central blind-ending branch of the lymphatic system called a *lacteal.* It has been calculated that this arrangement increases the surface area six hundred fold over that of a straight tube of the same dimension and length. The surface area of the small intestine is about 200m^2 in the average adult.

After a meal, as the activity of the cells in the small intestine increases, so too does their blood supply. At rest, the blood supply will be about 1.5 litres per minute, and it can easily increase by one third during digestion and absorption.

Each villus is supplied by fine branches from the internal nerve plexuses, and from the autonomic nervous system.

A small amount of smooth muscle tissue is present in the wall, which means that the villi can carry out free movement in addition to that which will occur mechanically with the passage of the gut contents. During digestion, the villi contract irregularly but quite quickly, thus helping to pump the circulating lymph in the lacteals. Some authorities postulate that a hormone – villikinin – is produced by the intestinal mucosa to stimulate this movement.

At the bases of the villi are the Crypts of Lieberkühn – tubular glands that secrete some of the intestinal fluid, bicarbonates and mucus. The stimulus for their secretion appears to be mechanical.

Here, at the bases of the villi, the cells have a very high rate of mitosis. Because of the amount of friction and wear and tear to which the intestine is subjected, worn-out cells are continuously being shed from the tips of the villi into the lumen of the gut, to be excreted in the faeces. About 250g of cell debris are thus expelled every day. The dividing cells in the bases of the crypts appear to migrate up the villi to replace those being shed. Because of the rapid rate of mitosis in this area, the epithelium is particularly susceptible to ionising radiation and other factors which might affect cell division, e.g. cytotoxic drugs. It is often quoted that the whole of the lining of the gut is replaced once every 36 hours. This is perhaps a somewhat unfortunate statement, since to the untutored it may conjure up the impression that the gut lining departs from the body like a rather long sleeve! An alarming thought.

Goblet cells that secrete mucus are also present at intervals over the surface of the villi. Lymphocytes are present throughout the small intestine in the mucosa – frequently grouped into lymph follicles that appear in the ileum as Peyer's patches.

It is interesting to note that in starvation it is not the stomach that shrinks, despite the old wives' tales; it is, in fact, the villi. In general, the villi (as described earlier) are about 1mm in height; after a period of starvation, the enterocytes – the epithelial cells that cover the surface of the villi – both shrink and decrease in number. Thus, the height of the villus decreases by up to half. Similarly, in coeliac disease the villi become stunted.

Intestinal juice (succus entericus)

It used to be thought that the 3000ml of intestinal juice produced each day by the glands in the crypts was rich in digestive enzymes. It now appears that the enzymes are actually produced from the disintegrating enterocytes shed from the tips of the villi (as described above), and are then mixed with the crypt secretion.

The secretion of the crypt glands is particularly rich in mucus. This is stimulated by the *nervi erigentes* of the parasympathetic nervous system. The amount of mucus secreted from these glands and from the goblet cells appears to increase in emotional disturbances. Normally, this mucus protects the gut wall and helps to bind the faeces.

The stimulus for secretion appears to be acid chyme entering the duodenum, as well as distension of the gut wall and impulses from the internal plexuses mediated via the vagus. It is possible that there is also hormonal stimulation by a substance called enterocrinin secreted from the intestinal mucosa.

The enzymes secreted by these cells are as follows:

1) *Peptidases* – mainly dipeptidase and aminopeptidases.
These act on amino acid sections – peptides – and split them into single absorbable amino acids.

2) *Amylase*
A small amount is secreted to break down any remaining carbohydrates to disaccharides.

3) *Maltase, sucrase and lactase*
These split the disaccharides maltose, sucrose and lactose into the monosaccharides glucose, fructose and galactose.

4) *Intestinal lipase*
This splits any remaining neutral fat (triglycerides) into fatty acids and glycerol.

By now, digestion is complete and one of the major functions of the gastrointestinal tract is accomplished. It now remains for absorption of the amino acids, monosaccharides, fatty acids, glycerol, vitamins, minerals and about 8.5 litres of water to take place.

Absorption
In general, this occurs by active transport or facilitated diffusion. The process is complicated and is not, as yet, fully understood.

1) *Carbohydrates*
These are actively transported (i.e. the process involves expending energy) across from the epithelium of the villi into the capillary network and thence into the portal circulation. It is thought that sodium is necessary for this to occur, as sodium and the monosaccharides seem to combine with a carrier molecule in the cell membrane to facilitate transport. This is usually completed in the jejunum.

2) *Proteins*
These, too, are actively carried across from the villi to the capillaries. There appear to be several different carriers involved, some of which may be congenitally deficient. Amino acids are absorbed very rapidly. Sodium appears to be necessary here, too, for transport to occur.

3) *Fats*
The micelles, together with fat-soluble vitamins, enter the epithelial cells of the villi. Inside the cells, the fatty acids and glycerol are resynthesised into triglycerides (neutral fat). These become enclosed in a layer of protein and lecithin to form chylomicrons and, as such, enter the central lacteal of each villus. The creamy fluid so formed (chyle) enters the lymphatic circulation and eventually is drained into the systemic venous circulation via the thoracic duct. Some short chain fatty acids are absorbed directly into the portal circulation. This accounts for 10–20 per cent of the total fat absorbed.

4) *Water and electrolytes*
Sodium and chloride are actively absorbed in large amounts in the small intestine. Calcium, potassium, iron, magnesium, phosphate and bicarbonate will also be absorbed here (see later for details of iron and

calcium absorption). Water is absorbed by osmosis at the rate of about 200–400ml/hour. It should be noted that in this region water can also pass in the opposite direction from blood to gut when the gut contents are hypertonic. This can be seen in dumping syndrome, after major gastric surgery and also with obstruction of the small intestine. In both cases, there is a marked increase in the osmolarity of the gut contents, and so water passes into the gut with a resultant eventual decrease in blood volume. Bile salts are absorbed and recirculated from the terminal ileum.

5) *Vitamin B_{12}*
In order for absorption of this vitamin to occur in the terminal ileum, it must form a complex with intrinsic factor secreted by the parietal cells of the stomach, as mentioned earlier. In the absence of this factor, only very small amounts of vitamin B_{12} can be absorbed and pernicious anaemia results. Vitamin B_{12} is stored by the liver in amounts sufficient to last the body for two to three years.

6) *Iron*
Absorption of iron occurs in the ileum. Bile salts appear to be necessary for its efficient absorption but, even so, only a fraction of the intake is absorbed each day. The actual amount appears to be regulated by the cells lining the small intestine. The cells contain iron, and when the body has a positive iron balance they absorb only small amounts. When the body's iron balance is negative (e.g. after a haemorrhage), their own iron stores are depleted and so these cells increase iron absorption.

7) *Calcium*
Calcium is poorly absorbed from the gut because it tends to form insoluble compounds which are not amenable to transport across the gut wall. However, calcium can be absorbed with relative ease in the presence of vitamin D, as this acts directly on the villi and increases the amount of the carrier which is required for calcium transport. Parathyroid hormone similarly exerts a direct effect in the small intestine to increase calcium absorption.

The major proportion of the daily calcium intake is excreted in the faeces, although a little is excreted in the urine. Parathyroid hormone influences the amount of calcium excreted via these routes, according to the body's need.

By the time the above-mentioned substances have been absorbed (about 9 hours after the food was ingested), the volume of remaining substances has decreased to between 500 and 1000ml, and it has the consistency of thin porridge. Tables 2.6, 2.7 and 2.8 summarise carbohydrate, protein and fat digestion.

THE LARGE INTESTINE

This 500–1000ml of chyme enters the large intestine laterally via the ileo-caecal valve. This valve has two horizontal folds which project into the caecum, the whole being made up of circular muscle fibres. The valve opens in response to peristaltic waves bringing the chyme towards it. The functions of the valve, like that of the pyloric sphincter, is to prevent the chyme leaving the small intestine with undue haste. It therefore controls the rate of flow and, in addition, prevents backflow.

The lumen of the large intestine is about 6–7cm in diameter and, apart from the stomach, it is the widest part of the tract. It has no villi, however, and for this reason has a much smaller surface area than the small intestine. Its width means that it is capable of storing and concentrating food residues, and movement throughout this area is much slower than in proximal areas of the gut.

The large intestine is about 1.5m long and consists of:
1) *The caecum* which is a blind-ending pouch into which the ileo-caecal valve empties. The pouch is about 7cm long.
2) *The appendix* which is vermiform (worm-like) and about the size of the little finger. It is made up of lymphoid tissue, and has no function in man. The appendix projects from the end of the caecum.
3) *The ascending colon* on the right of the abdomen, extending to the lower borders of the liver.
4) *The transverse colon,* dipping below the liver and stomach.
5) *The descending colon* on the left of the abdomen, giving rise to the S-shaped sigmoid colon which empties into
6) *The rectum,* which terminates in
7) *The anal canal,* which opens via sphincters to the exterior.

The large intestine produces no enzymes, and its only secretion appears to be mucus – necessary for the lubrication of the contents during their slow passage through this area, for the protection of the gut wall and for binding the faeces.

THE COLON

From the point of view of gut function, the colon is the area of the large

Table 2.6   Carbohydrate digestion.

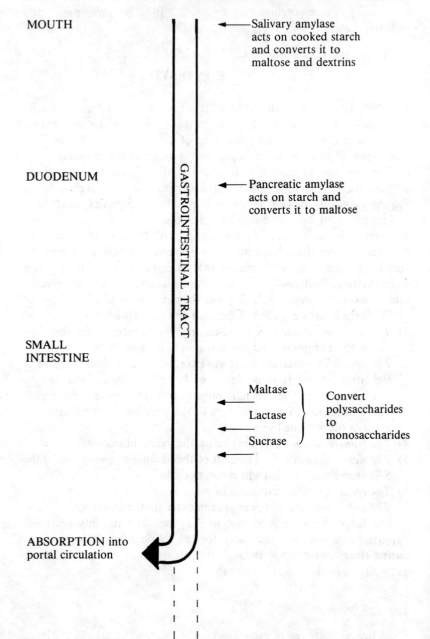

Table 2.7   Protein digestion.

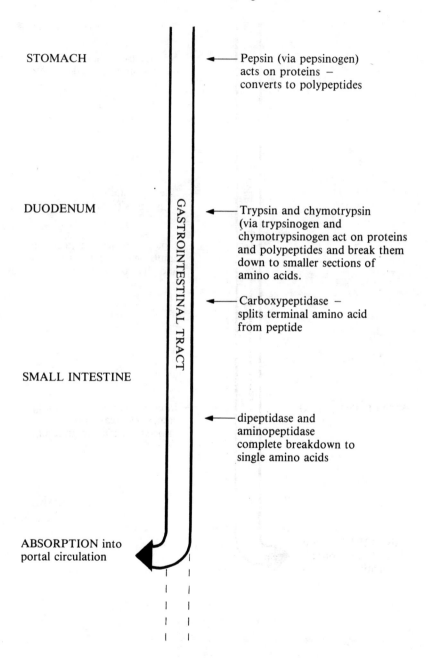

STOMACH

Pepsin (via pepsinogen)
acts on proteins –
converts to polypeptides

DUODENUM

GASTROINTESTINAL TRACT

Trypsin and chymotrypsin
(via trypsinogen and
chymotrypsinogen act on proteins
and polypeptides and break them
down to smaller sections of
amino acids.

Carboxypeptidase –
splits terminal amino acid
from peptide

SMALL INTESTINE

dipeptidase and
aminopeptidase
complete breakdown to
single amino acids

ABSORPTION into
portal circulation

Table 2.8   Neutral fat digestion.

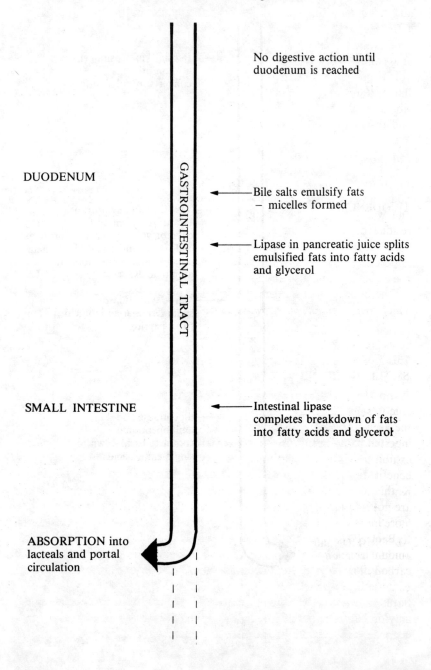

No digestive action until
duodenum is reached

DUODENUM

GASTROINTESTINAL TRACT

Bile salts emulsify fats
– micelles formed

Lipase in pancreatic juice splits
emulsified fats into fatty acids
and glycerol

SMALL INTESTINE

Intestinal lipase
completes breakdown of fats
into fatty acids and glycerol

ABSORPTION into
lacteals and portal
circulation

intestine that is of the most interest. Once more, structure is modified to fit function: the walls of the colon show adaptation from the basic four-layered model previously described. In the walls of the colon, the longitudinal muscle bands are incomplete, and are gathered into three flat bands called the *taenia coli*. Between the taenia, the wall of the colon pouches outwards to form haustra (Latin 'buckets'). The haustrations are produced by the contraction of the circular muscle fibres. As the haustra fill and empty, they aid kneading of the contents and absorption.

Functions of the colon

1) *Absorption of sodium and water*
Sodium is actively transported from the lumen to the portal circulation, and water follows. The amount of water absorbed from the colonic residue depends on the length of time it remains in the colon. The longer it remains, the drier will be the faeces. Water absorption is an important function of the colon. Certain drugs – aspirin, steroids, some anaesthetics – and also amino acids may be absorbed colonically.

The bulk of the faecal matter is made up of cellulose – a substance which man is unable to digest, since he lacks the vital enzyme cellulase.

2) *Secretion of mucus* (see page 41)
This gives the contents of the colon a pH of about 8.

3) *Incubation of bacteria* – Bacteroides, streptococci and lactobacilli.
Due to slow movement through the colon, bacteria are able to colonise the area. In a baby, the gut is initially sterile, but within a few days ingested bacteria invade and colonise the area. Many of these bacteria exhibit a symbiotic relationship with man: that is, they derive mutual benefit. In exchange for food and shelter, the bacteria produce vitamin K, thiamine and riboflavin in small amounts. Normally, these amounts are not significant, but in times of vitamin deficiency they can become more important.

Bacterial fermentation produces flatus in the colon in quite large amounts: 500–700ml may be produced each day, consisting of nitrogen, carbon dioxide, hydrogen, methane and hydrogen sulphide. Intestinal bacteria in cows are much more efficient, producing up to 600 litres of flatus each day. The amounts of flatus produced in man depends not only on bacterial activity but also on the food eaten: baked beans, for instance, are capable of increasing by tenfold the amount of flatus produced. Indole and skatole are two of the products of amine breakdown which give the faeces their characteristic odour. These products arise from bacterial decomposition.

Movements of the colon
Contraction of the circular muscle in the colon results in segmentation. Segments of the colon about 20cm long appear to be filled at a time. Contractions occur perhaps once every half-hour, moving the contents of one segment on to the next. Thus, the contents remain within the colon for a long time – anything up to 24 hours. This type of movement can be considered as non-propulsive, and is the major movement of constipated patients.

Two or three times a day, usually after meals, an increase in activity occurs in the colon. After meals, especially the first meal of the day, the gastro-colic reflex occurs: the ileum becomes increasingly contractile, and contraction of the terminal ileum causes the ileo-colic sphincter to relax, so filling the caecum and colon.

Associated with this, the phenomenon of 'mass movement' occurs within the colon, propelling the mid-colonic contents towards the rectum. The haustrations disappear from the mid-colon. The tube becomes shortened and flattened by waves of rapidly advancing powerful contractions, and the contents of the colon are moved at speed (indeed, within a few seconds) into the descending sigmoid colon. Until the faeces actually enter the rectum, the subject is not aware of these movements.

THE RECTUM

The rectum is usually empty until just before defaecation. It consists of a muscular distensible tube 12–15cm long, which receives the 100–150g of faeces usually eliminated daily. This material consists of 30–50g of solids and 70–100g of water. The solid components are made up of cellular debris, undigested food substances (principally cellulose), dead bacteria, bile pigments (stercobilin), a little sodium and some potassium. It seems that a small amount of potassium is actually secreted into the colon – a fact of some significance in diarrhoea, when quite large amounts may be lost from the body.

Mass movement of the colon, described earlier, suddenly distends the rectal walls. This initiates the 'call to stool', and the subject becomes aware of the need to defaecate. Afferent impulses travel to the defaecation centre in the sacral spinal cord. In adults, defaecation is under voluntary control, and the defaecation centre is permitted (if appropriate) to initiate expulsion of faeces. If defaecation is inconvenient, the sacral centre can be inhibited by the cerebral cortex.

Defaecation is accomplished in some measure by straining; the degree to which this is necessary depends on the consistency of the faeces. Peristalsis of the sigmoid colon contributes to the process. In straining, the intra-abdominal pressure is raised by contracting the abdominal muscles and expiring against a closed glottis. This causes the pressure in the rectum to rise to about 200mm Hg. The net result of these defaecatory actions is that blood pressure rises and then suddenly falls with the decrease in venous return. Thus it is not unheard of for the call to stool to precipitate a pulmonary embolism, cerebral-vascular accident or coronary thrombosis in those susceptible.

The anal canal is emptied by contracting the *levator ani muscles,* with relaxation of the internal and external anal sphincters which guard the exit. The internal sphincter is composed of smooth muscle and is thus not under voluntary control. The external anal sphincter, conversely, is under the control of the will, being composed of striated muscle.

Apart from this control of the urge to defaecate, and the initial decision to ingest and swallow food – both under the control of the will – what goes on in the portion of the gut between the oesophagus and rectum is completely involuntary, and to a lot of people incomprehensible or rarely considered.

It is, however, something of a marvel that every day we consume approximately one kilo (two pounds) of foodstuffs, together with about two litres of fluids and without conscious effort or thought, the gastrointestinal tract mashes it up, squirts enzymes on it, digests it, takes out the nutrients and water, and expels the residue to the exterior without problems.

It is with some of the problems that *can* occur that the rest of this book is concerned.

REFERENCES

Guyton 1977. *Basic Human Physiology – Normal Function and Mechanisms of Disease.* 2nd edition. Saunders.

Lippold and Winton 1979. *Human Physiology* 7th edition. Churchill Livingstone.

Pansky, B. 1975. *Dynamic Anatomy and Physiology.* New York; Macmillan.

Russell, Myles and de Coursey 1977. *The Human Organism* 4th edition. McGraw-Hill.

QUESTIONS FOR DISCUSSION

The following items are included to help you to check on your understanding of the material presented in this chapter. Please read each question carefully.

In each case, there is at least one correct answer and at least one incorrect answer (i.e. in no case are all of the alternatives correct or all of them incorrect).

If you are unsure of your answer, go back to the text and reread the appropriate section, where the answer can be found.

1) Which of the following statements concerning the wall of the gut is true?
   a) blood vessels are contained within the serous layer,
   b) the mucosal layer is secretory,
   c) the muscle layer contains neurones,
   d) lymph follicles are absent from the submucosa.

2) The following statements all concern the nervous regulation of the gut. Which are true?
   a) the vagus supplies the whole of the large intestine,
   b) there is no sympathetic innervation to the gut,
   c) parasympathetic stimulation results in excitation of the gut wall,
   d) all the sphincters are under voluntary control.

3) There is one incorrect statement in these assertions about the stomach. What is it?
   a) at rest, the volume of the stomach is about 50ml,
   b) about 20 per cent of ingested alcohol is absorbed there,
   c) intragastric pressure is subatmospheric,
   d) the pyloric sphincter is formed of circular and longitudinal fibres only.

4) Study the following statements about gastric secretion. Which of them are true?

   a) adults secrete adequate amounts of rennin for curd formation,
   b) mucus secretion is sufficient to produce a 1mm thick mucus lining to the stomach,
   c) parietal cells contain carbonic acid which facilitates bicarbonate production,
   d) hydrochloric acid inactivates salivary amylase.

5) Which of the following are secreted by the cells of the pancreas?

   a) glycogen,
   b) bicarbonate,
   c) enterokinase,
   d) chymotrypsinogen.

6) Which of the following statements about pancreatic secretion are true?

   a) it occurs as a result of gastric distension,
   b) secretin induces a secretion rich in pancreatic enzymes,
   c) CCK–PZ secretion occurs as a result of glucose entering the duodenum,
   d) both secretin and CCK–PZ inhibit gastric secretion.

7) Which of these substances can be found in bile?

   a) ferritin,
   b) stercobilinogen,
   c) cholesterol,
   d) vitamin A.

8) Which of the following statements about the small intestine are correct?

   a) at rest, the blood supply is about 3 litres/min,
   b) each villus is capable of independent movement,
   c) the surface area is roughly equivalent to one square metre per kg of body weight,
   d) the villi shrink in starvation.

9) If an ileostomy is performed, which of the following functions may be interfered with?

   a) iron absorption,
   b) intrinsic factor secretion,
   c) micelle formation,
   d) bicarbonate reabsorption.

10) The following statements concern the colon. Which are correct?

   a) haustrations aid in kneading the colon contents,
   b) sodium is actively absorbed in this region,

    c) muscle contractions occur once each minute,
    d) man normally produces about 3 litres of flatus each day.

11) Defaecation normally occurs as a result of:
    a) mass movement of the colon,
    b) a rise in intra-rectal pressure to 20mm Hg,
    c) relaxing the abdominal muscles and expiring against a closed glottis,
    d) contraction of the *levator ani* muscles.

Chapter 3

Bowel Stomas:
Why and How they are Created

Stoma is a word derived from the Greek and means a mouth or opening. A stoma is constructed from a portion of the large or small bowel, brought to the surface through a surgical incision, and varying in size and length according to its position and intended function. The normal colour of a healthy stoma is a pinkish red, which may be compared to the colour of the inside lining of the mouth.

CONDITIONS FOR WHICH BOWEL STOMAS ARE RAISED

These may be further divided into conditions which require temporary colostomy, permanent colostomy or ileostomy.

TEMPORARY COLOSTOMY

1) Acute intestinal obstruction – due to cancer of the left colon or rectum. A loop colostomy is the most usual emergency procedure. Anterior resection, anastamosis and closure of the colostomy may follow subsequently.
2) Diverticulitis – inflammation of diverticula in the bowel wall, with the risk of abscess formation and perforation of the gut. A temporary transverse colostomy is raised as a first stage, followed by further operations to remove the diseased portion of colon and ultimately to restore continuity of bowel function.
3) Volvulus – a twisted loop of gut which causes acute obstruction. Immediate surgery is required to relieve the obstruction and a temporary colostomy is often performed to protect the operation site.
4) Hirschsprung's disease – congenital paralysis of the lower bowel

and rectum, and congenital malformation or absence of the rectum or anus in infants, all require an emergency colostomy raised within days of birth. A loop colostomy in the right transverse colon is normally raised. Reconstructive surgery may take place later. (See Chapter 9.)

5) Recto-vaginal and recto-vesical fistulae – with the danger of infection and obstruction, both require the faecal stream to be diverted by a temporary colostomy so that eventually further surgery can be performed in a clean field.

6) High fistula – in-ano and perianal abscess – both these disorders are difficult to treat without the formation of a temporary colostomy proximal to the infected area. A double-barrelled sigmoid colostomy is often formed to divert the faecal stream.

7) Trauma to the left colon and ano-rectal wounds – the immediate raising of a transverse colostomy is done as an emergency procedure, and reconstructive surgery can then be attempted later on. This type of injury can occur as the result of road traffic accidents, impalement on railings or similar, or as a consequence of stabbing or shooting incidents.

8) Resection and anastamosis of the left colon and upper rectum – it is necessary for the faecal stream to be diverted by a temporary transverse colostomy in order to protect the anastamosis and allow it to heal firmly.

9) Post-irradiation conditions, e.g. proctitis, stricture, etc. – may require diversion of faeces by colostomy.

PERMANENT COLOSTOMY

1) rectal cancer – treated by abdomino-perineal resection and the formation of a permanent sigmoid colostomy.

2) Anal cancer – a permanent sigmoid end colostomy is formed after excision of the tumour.

3) Irreparable trauma to the rectum – this will necessitate removal of the rectum and the formation of an end colostomy in the descending or sigmoid colon.

4) Rectal prolapse – which cannot successfully be corrected surgically – is treated by excision of the rectum and the formation of a terminal colostomy in the sigmoid colon.

5) Cancer of the recto-sigmoid zone – if the condition of the patient does not warrant removal of the rectum, an end colostomy will be formed in the upper sigmoid colon.

6) Injuries or abnormalities of the spinal cord – paralysis of the anal

sphincter and resultant faecal incontinence requires the formation of a permanent colostomy to end the misery of constant soiling.

ILEOSTOMY

1) Ulcerative colitis. This is a non-specific inflammatory disease of the colon and rectum, occurring most commonly in persons between the ages of twenty and forty years, and is of unknown cause. Total colectomy and excision of the rectum (pan-proctocolectomy) may be required ultimately, and a permanent ileostomy made.
N.B. The ileostomy may be temporary and followed by an operation for ileo-rectal anastamosis and closure of the stoma. This procedure is attempted where the rectum is clear of the disease, but regular follow-up is necessary due to the high risk of developing cancer in the preserved rectum.

2) Crohn's disease – a chronic granulomatous inflammatory condition which can occur at any point throughout the gastro-intestinal tract and is of uncertain cause. This disease affects mainly the same age groups as ulcerative colitis. If Crohn's disease occurs in the colon and ileum, the thickening of the bowel wall, abscess and fistula formation and obstruction may make pan-proctocolectomy with excision of the affected terminal ileum necessary, and a permanent ileostomy will be raised.

3) Familial polyposis coli – a pre-malignant condition in which polypi are present in the rectum and pelvic colon. In some cases the polypi are profuse and widespread, and pan-proctocolectomy with formation of a permanent ileostomy is the operative technique employed.
N.B. Many cases of Familial polyposis coli are managed by sub-total removal of the affected colon and anastamosis of the terminal ileum to the rectal stump, thus avoiding the formation of a stoma.

4) Cancer of the colon or rectum, or both – malignancy may develop in persons with chronic ulcerative colitis, at any age and at any stage of the disease. Total removal of colon and rectum and permanent ileostomy is indicated.

5) Entero-colitis – is a rare granulomatous disease which can affect both colon and ileum. The disease may be seen in infants and is a reason for colectomy and ileostomy in very young babies. It is always hoped that ileo-rectal anastamosis will be possible later on if the child thrives and gains weight.

6) Fulminating amoebiasis – a condition which causes dysentery, liver abscess and toxic megacolon. This condition is seen mainly in the

so-called Third World and seldom presents in the Western hemisphere. A relieving small bowel stoma may be required as a temporary measure.

TYPES OF STOMA

1) A *permanent end (terminal)* colostomy may be sited at any level within the colon and on any part of the abdominal wall. The most usual site is in the left lower quadrant of the abdomen, exteriorising the sigmoid or descending colon (see Figure 3.1). The most common reasons for a permanent end colostomy are:
a) following resection of part of the colon and the whole of the rectum;
b) following Hartmann's procedure involving oversewing the rectal stump and exteriorisation of the proximal stoma at any level within the colon.

Ideally, a permanent colostomy should protrude above the abdominal skin surface for at least 0.5cm and be about 2.5cm in diameter, but there are many patients with healthily functioning bowel stomas which differ quite considerably from these ideal measurements. Any gross deviation in size, shape, colour or function should be noted immediately however, and appropriate action taken by the surgeon.

A 'continent' permanent colostomy involves the implantation of a magnetic ring which is sutured subcutaneously into the abdominal wall under a flush end colostomy. The stoma cover consists of a magnetic cap with central plug to fit the stoma precisely. This type of stoma is only suitable for selected patients and the technique may still be considered experimental.

Temporary colostomies may be raised at almost any point in the colon, but are most commonly raised in the transverse colon. The right transverse colon is the elective field for a temporary colostomy, as the colon is mobile at this site and can be brought to the surface easily. This type of stoma is fashioned when the disease or injury is such that it will be possible to restore the continuity of the colon at a subsequent operation.

2) A *loop* colostomy is the most common temporary colostomy. A section of the right transverse colon is brought out through a transverse incision, supported on the body surface by a rod or bridge, opened longitudinally and the edges of the mucosa sutured to the skin edges (see Chapter 6, Figure 6.3).

3) A *Paul Mikulicz* variety of temporary stoma is formed by suturing

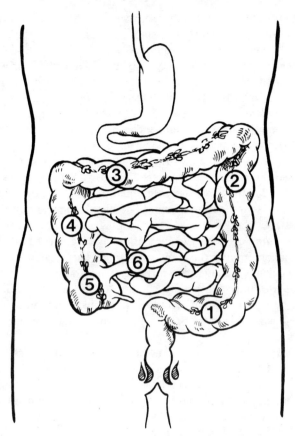

Figure 3.1   Types of stoma and typical sites.

Stoma	Colon removed or by-passed	Type of effluent
1. Sigmoid colostomy	Part of sigmoid colon and whole of rectum	Firm, solid, separate stool
2. Descending colostomy	Descending colon below splenic flexure and whole of rectum	Formed stool
3. Transverse colostomy, doubled-barrelled or loop	All of the colon and rectum distal to the stoma	Semi-liquid
4. Ascending colostomy	All of the colon and rectum distal to the stoma	Semi-liquid
5. Caecostomy	All of the colon and rectum distal to the stoma	Liquid
6. Ileostomy	Usually the entire colon and rectum	Liquid and continuous

the two ends of the colon together for several inches inside the abdomen to make a spur. Ultimately the spur is crushed by enterotome, and continuity of bowel action is resumed without further operation.

4) A *double-barrelled* colostomy may be fashioned by bringing the proximal and distal ends of the divided colon to the surface to form two stomas, which may be close together or separated by a skin 'bridge'. This type of stoma may be sited in the transverse colon, or in the sigmoid region through an oblique incision.

5) A *Devine's* colostomy is raised in cases where it is essential that there is no faecal spillage into the distal, or defunctioning, end of the colon. For this operation the colon is divided, and the two ends brought out of the abdominal wall separately and at some distance from each other, to form two separate stomas. The distal stoma is described as a mucous fistula.

6) An *ascending* colostomy is comparatively rare but may be required to relieve a condition of the transverse colon. This type of stoma in the ascending colon is managed similarly to an ileostomy.

7) A *caecostomy* is an opening made into the caecum during emergency surgery in order to decompress the distended gut. The acute intestinal obstruction may be due to volvulus of the pelvic colon or caecum.

8) An *ileostomy* is a stoma of the small bowel and is constructed by bringing the terminal ileum through a small incision in the abdominal wall, most usually sited on the lower right side of the abdomen. The withdrawn length of terminal small bowel is everted and sutured into position forming a 'spout'. Ideally, this spout should measure not less than 2.5cm and not more than 5cm. After pan-proctocolectomy an ileostomy is a permanent stoma, although ileostomy with a colonic mucous fistula may be constructed as a temporary defunctioning procedure, with subsequent closure of the ileostomy and resumption of normal faecal flow. Closure of an ileostomy and ileo-rectal anastamosis would only be considered for patients where the preserved rectum was completely clear of inflammatory disease, and is never attempted in cases of carcinoma or Crohn's disease.

9) *Kock pouch.* Mention must be made of the operation devised by Professor Nils Kock, whereby a reservoir and valve are fashioned from the terminal ileum inside the abdomen. The surface opening connects to the reservoir by means of the valve, and a catheter is used to empty the pouch several times a day. This operation would only be considered suitable for carefully selected patients with ulcerative colitis, and not for those suffering from Crohn's disease or carcinoma. The concept of a

continent ileostomy is an attractive one and refinements of the surgical techniques involved are helping to overcome some of the complications which can arise.

REFERENCES

Todd, Ian P. (ed.) 1978. *Intestinal Stomas.* Heinemann.
Frobisher, Martin, *et al.* 1964. *Microbiology for Nurses* 11th edition. Saunders.
Shafer, Newton K. 1979. *Medical-surgical Nursing* 6th edition. Mosby.
Walker, Frank C. (ed.) 1976. *Modern Stoma Care.* Churchill Livingstone.

QUESTIONS FOR DISCUSSION

1) Mention three diseases or conditions for which a temporary colostomy would be raised, and indicate what further surgery might be contemplated.
2) Mention three conditions requiring the formation of a permanent colostomy and the operative procedures indicated.
3) What is the commonest condition necessitating the formation of an ileostomy, and where would a permanent ileostomy most usually be sited?
4) What is the argument against the formation of a temporary ileostomy in a patient with ulcerative colitis?
5) Discuss the differences between the normal siting of a permanent sigmoid colostomy and a temporary loop colostomy.
6) What type of effluent is to be expected from a colostomy sited in the transverse colon?
7) Describe the formation of a double-barrelled colostomy and state where it may be sited.

Chapter 4

The Practical Management of Bowel Stomas

The management of bowel stomas is normally a comparatively simple and straightforward series of practical procedures, which can be readily adapted to satisfy the individual needs of each patient at every stage of post-operative recovery and rehabilitation.

PRE-OPERATIVE COUNSELLING

Whenever possible, it is important that each prospective stoma patient is interviewed before surgery by a nurse trained in all the aspects of stoma care, so that full and informed answers can be given to the many questions which occur to the patient, and some of the inevitable fears and worries alleviated to some extent. At this time, suitable types of appliance can be demonstrated and discussed, and information given about after-care facilities, sources of help, the obtaining of supplies, financial considerations, and the many booklets and practical aid leaflets freely available. The possibility of a pre-operative visit from an established ostomist of the same sex and comparable life-style can be suggested, and arranged if the patient agrees. This living proof of successful resumption of a normal life is often very reassuring. All this information is of great value, but probably the most significantly comforting factor in the pre-operative counselling sessions is the patient's knowledge that expert support, both practical and emotional, is readily available for as long as it is required, and that every effort will be made to find acceptable solutions to any problems which may arise. Wherever practicable, it is helpful to involve a close member of the patient's family in the pre-operative discussions, so that the process of reintegration into the family circle after operation will be made more confidently and without embarrassment. Assurance can also be given to the majority of patients who live alone that they will be able to resume their normal independent lifestyle after stoma surgery.

SITING OF STOMAS

Before the advent of nurses specially trained in all aspects of stoma care, the siting of permanent stomas was left to the surgeon concerned, and was often decided when the patient was already anaesthetised and lying supine on the operating table. This lack of pre-operative siting of the stoma, whether for colostomy or ileostomy, frequently resulted in the stoma placement being unsuitable and inconvenient, and caused unnecessary problems of management for the patient. The stoma care nurse is often asked by the consultant surgeon to mark the site for the stoma during a pre-operative visit to the patient, or the site could be decided upon by the surgeon and stoma care nurse together during a ward round. In situations where there is no stoma care nurse in post, the site might be marked pre-operatively by an experienced ward sister, perhaps with the co-operation of a surgical registrar. The importance of carefully considering the best possible stoma site for each individual patient cannot be over-stressed (see Figure 4.1). The illustrated section

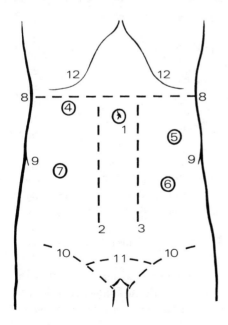

Figure 4.1   Stoma sites.

1. Umbilicus.
2. Right paramedian incision.
3. Left paramedian incision.
4. Transverse colostomy.
5. Descending colostomy.
6. Sigmoid colostomy.
7. Ileostomy.
8. Waistline.
9. Hip bones.
10. Groin crease.
11. Symphysis pubis.
12. Rib cage.

between pages 190 and 191 shows not only suitable stoma sites but also actual and potential problem sites for stomas.

It is essential to assess the general physique of the patient who is to have stoma surgery. Note must be taken of the degree of obesity or emaciation present and also of height and normal posture.

Wherever possible a stoma should be sited to avoid:

1) The umbilical depression; .
2) The bony prominence of either hip;
3) Drainage holes, or holes caused by previous injury;
4) The natural waistline, and any fatty folds in this area;
5) The operative incision and any other scars, e.g. appendicectomy scar near an ileostomy site, or the scar resulting from repair of a left inguinal hernia near a possible colostomy site;
6) The groin flexure on either side;
7) Any fatty bulges, and the deep creases caused by movement of these bulges;
8) Areas affected by chronic skin conditions e.g. psoriasis;
9) Supporting straps attached to an artificial limb;
10) Any other surgical appliance, e.g. truss.

It is important to have the full co-operation of an alert patient who is able to adopt various positions, sitting, standing and reclining, so that he can feel that he has helped to decide the best stoma site to suit his own individual needs.

Grossly obese patients pose a particular problem, as there may be considerable weight loss after surgery, and the site first chosen for the stoma could subsequently prove to be too low. Generally speaking, it is advisable to site the stoma on an obese patient slightly higher than usual, and to mark it on the upper slope of the bulge. If this is not done, there is a risk of the stoma sinking into a flabby groove and almost disappearing from view.

Conversely, when marking the site for an ileostomy on a frail and very underweight colitic patient, it must be remembered that there is likely to be a dramatic weight gain and general 'filling-out' after a successful operation, and this must be allowed for in the pre-operative siting.

In addition to the above considerations, careful attention should be paid to the normal life-style of the patient, the type of work to which he will return, hobbies, sport or other recreational activities, and the preferred styles of clothing habitually worn. Physical abnormalities and conditions such as arthritis, poor eyesight, loss of a limb or muscular degeneration, must also be considered, together with any mental handicap or psychiatric disorder.

It can be seen, therefore, that pre-operative counselling and marking of the preferred stoma site is of the greatest importance, and should be routine procedure in all cases of elective stoma surgery.

APPLIANCE MANAGEMENT

With every type of bowel stoma it is necessary to have some simple and efficient method of collecting the faecal effluent which flows from them, involuntarily and at any time. There are many different styles of appliances and accessories available, and care must be taken to select the correct one for every individual patient. The chosen appliance would need to be of adequate size to contain the volume of effluent, of a suitable style, odourproof, with an adhesive which does not cause an allergic reaction, and one which is easy for the patient to manage alone.

Obviously all types of appliance require regular changing, and an acceptable routine should be established to help every patient to become adept in his own stoma care. It is not possible to make hard and fast rules about the frequency with which stoma bags should be changed, as this has to be dictated by so many different circumstances. It is reasonable, however, to change a drainable appliance every three to four days, providing that no abnormality of the stoma or its effluent is observed through the transparent plastic of the bag and that no discomfort is felt by the patient. If any leakage occurs, however slight, the appliance must be changed immediately. Two-piece appliances comprising a Stomahesive flange and a clip-on bag may be left in place for the same length of time, whether the bag is drainable or closed, as the bag can be changed at will and the protective flange left in place. Constant and unnecessary stripping off of an adhesive appliance from an unprotected skin is to be avoided at all times.

BASIC REQUIREMENTS FOR AN APPLIANCE CHANGE

1) New appliance of correct size and type;
2) Stoma measuring guide;
3) Micropore tape 25mm width;
4) Any individual requirements such as Stomahesive, barrier creams, skin gel, deodorant or medical adhesive;
5) Soft paper tissues and unsterile gauze squares;

6) Disposal bag or newspaper for soiled material;
7) Warm water;
8) Spare closure clip for drainable appliance;
9) Scissors – preferably with one rounded and one pointed end;
109 Portable mirror – e.g. make-up or shaving mirror with stand;
11) Plastic box with lid, or covered tray, to hold each patient's own requirements for his stoma care. This container should be kept at the bedside in hospital.

It is usually more convenient for the nurse, and more comfortable and private for the patient, if the immediate post-operative appliance changes are done with the patient lying in or on his bed. It is essential that the nurse explains exactly what she is doing, and that she encourages the interest and co-operation of the patient in all aspects of dealing with his stoma.

BASIC ROUTINE FOR CHANGING AN APPLIANCE – BY THE NURSE

1) All necessary equipment should be brought to the bedside, including paper towels or other means of protecting the bed and the patient's clothes.
2) The bed should be screened and the patient told what is going to be done. Reassurance should be given that pain will not be caused.
3) The patient should be comfortable and relaxed. The abdomen is then uncovered and the bedclothes protected with paper towels.
4) A clean appliance is checked to see that it is the correct size and type and prepared for use.
5) If using Stomahesive, the hole should be cut to fit neatly around the stoma and the white backing paper left in situ until the time for application.
6) Four strips of adhesive tape about 10cm long may be cut ready for use.
7) The old appliance should be removed with care, peeling it off from the upper edge and easing the abdominal skin away with the other hand. Appliances should never be dragged straight off the skin, or damage will occur.
8) The stoma and skin should be wiped round gently with dry tissues to remove most of the faeces.
9) The stoma and surrounding area should be washed with gauze squares and warm water. Lotions and disinfectants need not be used but a mild soap may be necessary at times.
10) The skin should be dried thoroughly, and if a skin protective agent

is to be used it should be applied at this stage. Creams should be massaged into the skin until perfectly dry and non-greasy. Any surplus cream must be wiped off.

11) The stoma should be observed for any sign of discolouration, recession, prolapse or other abnormality. Any adverse signs must be reported to the ward sister or charge nurse.

12) The peristomal skin should be observed for redness or excoriation. Immediate steps should be taken to remedy these conditions with the use of Stomahesive or other barriers under the appliance.

13) The stoma should be measured in case the size or shape has altered. If necessary the size of the appliance should be changed.

14) The correct size and type of appliance should be fitted, ensuring that the adhesive flange is perfectly smooth and wrinkle-free, with the hole centred over the stoma. There should be about 3mm (⅛ inch) clearance all round the stoma whatever type of appliance is used. A little air should be introduced into a plastic bag, to prevent the surfaces sticking together and pressing on the stoma.

15) If using a drainable appliance, care should be taken to ensure that the clip or other closure is correctly applied and left in the closed position.

16) Any belt worn should be attached to the appliance and positioned level with the stoma, to avoid upward 'drag' and possible injury to the stoma.

BASIC ROUTINE FOR CHANGING AN APPLIANCE – BY THE PATIENT

When patients are changing their own appliances the basic requirements and method are the same as itemised in the sections on Basic Requirements and Basic Routine above. It is strongly recommended that equipment is kept together in a suitable container, and that a mirror is used to check that the appliance is correctly positioned.

For obvious reasons, the system of 'looking across' at the stoma in a mirror, rather than 'looking down', is particularly indicated for a female patient with a well-developed bust.

It is normally easier for a patient to stand, or to lean on the edge of a high stool while doing his own stoma care. Sitting on a low chair or half-reclining causes creases and wrinkles to appear on the abdominal surface, and makes it very difficult to achieve a perfectly positioned and leak-free fit of the chosen appliance.

DISPOSAL – IN HOSPITAL

The disposal of soiled appliances and dressings in hospital does not pose a problem, but correct procedures should be followed at all times.
1) A paper disposal bag is taken to the bedside with the other requirements for an appliance change. A small stock of similar bags should be kept with each patient's equipment when he commences to take care of his own stoma while still in hospital.
2) Soiled appliances should be emptied into a covered receptacle or directly into the sluice or toilet, before being deposited, with any other used dressings, into the disposal bag and thence into the Dirty Dressing container in the sluice area.

It does sometimes happen that disposal bags are put into the Dirty Dressing container complete with unemptied ostomy appliance. This careless habit is not only unpleasant but is also an infection risk.

Anyone, nurse or patient, involved in the changing and handling of used stoma appliances should remember to follow a routine hand-washing procedure afterwards.

DISPOSAL – AT HOME

Disposal of used appliances and dressings in the home is a much more difficult procedure for many patients, and is often a prime cause for concern when the time for discharge from hospital approaches. There is no universal simple solution to this particular problem and the procedure must be geared to suit the domestic circumstances of each individual. The best method for disposal of soiled bags is to burn them, after first emptying the contents into the toilet. These days very few people have any means of incineration, and the following method is the one more usually employed.
1) The contents of the bag are emptied into the toilet. A cut may be made in the bottom of a closed end bag to facilitate this procedure.
2) The appliance is rinsed well before being wrapped tightly in several layers of newspaper, preferably also sealed into a plastic or paper bag, and then placed into the dustbin.
N.B. It is often convenient and easy to utilise the flush of water into the toilet to rinse through the stoma bag.

Procedures 1) and 2) should also be followed when a rubbish chute, as provided in high rise apartment buildings, is used. It is essential that the waste material is firmly wrapped and sealed before being discarded.

Some areas provide a Dirty Dressing collection service, which may be used for the disposal of used ostomy appliances, though patients are often reluctant to be singled out as in need of such a service.

A special, closed, chemically treated waste disposal unit for bathroom or toilet, into which used appliances may be dropped, is available to ostomy patients at an approximate cost of sixty or seventy pounds annually. The commercial suppliers of these units operate a collection and replacement service every few weeks and cover most areas of Great Britain. (Ref. COMEX units, Messrs Cannon Hygiene Ltd, Carnforth.)

DISPOSAL – AWAY FROM HOME

When on holiday, or visiting away from home, the discreet disposal of soiled appliances may appear to pose a big problem. The same empty-rinse-wrap and seal routine should be followed, and an opportunity found to discard the parcel into a dustbin or other waste container. It is advisable always to use paper tissues or soft toilet paper for cleaning and drying purposes, as these are easily flushed away in the toilet and will not clog it.

It is highly inadvisable to dispose of soiled appliances by cutting them up and attempting to flush them away. This procedure may succeed the first time, but the waste pipes will rapidly become blocked with plastic and a great deal of embarrassment and unpleasantness will be the result.

ODOUR

The odour emanating from the faecal matter discharged from a bowel stoma is perfectly natural, and should be no more than would be experienced on evacuation of faeces from the anus. However, the fear of being the source of offensive odour worries most ostomists, and information on the steps to take to dispel this anxiety should be readily available.

1) *Appliances* – most of the modern disposable appliances are fashioned from odour-proof plastic material, and several of them incorporate a built-in charcoal filter to deodorise the escaping flatus. This type of appliance has an adhesive flange which bonds closely to the body, thus ensuring that there is no odour-producing leakage of faeces around the stoma.

2) *Deodorants* – there is a range of accessories produced to aid stoma

patients to overcome the odour problem. Special drops or powders may be instilled into each bag before use, and a fresh and pleasant-smelling aerosol spray can be used just before changing or emptying the appliance. On a more general level, household deodorant sprays and atomisers are helpful when used in the bathroom or toilet in the home.
3) *Diet* – odour and flatus-producing food and drink such as onions, beer, highly spiced foods or curries etc. are best avoided. Some patients find that chlorophyll or charcoal tablets taken before meals are of use (see Chapter 12).

Discarded soiled appliances should not become a source of odour if the correct procedure for disposal has been carefully followed (see 'Disposal', pages 64–5).

The most effective method of controlling odour is to have the right appliance, correctly fitted, and to make sure that scrupulous attention is paid to the basic rules of good personal hygiene and cleanliness.

BATHING

The fact that a person has a stoma is no bar to enjoying a bath or shower, and it is a matter of choice and convenience as to whether the appliance is removed during bathing. When bathing with the appliance in place it is wise to seal the edges of the flange with waterproof tape before immersion, to avoid loosening of the adhesive.

Ostomists who have achieved a relatively settled life-style will often know when a bath without a stoma covering can be taken, confident that there is a minimal risk of stomal action, but the majority tend to prefer to wear their usual bag at bathtime. There are several makes of small pouches or stoma caps, suitable for those people who like to apply a neater cover whilst bathing. As with most aspects of stoma care, it is a matter of personal choice, and a bath 'all over' without a bag on can be very refreshing.

Patients often need to be reassured that the bath water will not do their stoma any harm, and also that it will not get in through the hole and cause them to fill up with soapy liquid and sink!

CLOTHES

Normal clothing can be worn, and there is no need for ostomists to think that they are condemned to a lifetime of tent dresses and baggy trousers. It is obviously inadvisable for tight clothing of any kind to be worn in the immediate post-operative period, and care must always be taken to see that there is no direct pressure on the stoma itself.

1) *Men* – any chosen style of work or leisure clothes can be worn with the exception of tight hipster trousers, which are wrongly cut for the average ostomist. Sometimes there may be pressure problems with belts and trouser waistbands due to the position of the stoma, so that a change to wearing braces is advisable. Obese patients must avoid any tight bands around waist or abdomen, and constriction or pressure on the stoma at any time might result in serious damage.

Boxer style swimming trunks are best for swimming or sunbathing, and ordinary shorts resting on the natural waistline can be worn for other sporting activities.

2) *Women* – many women like to wear some sort of girdle or roll-on. This is perfectly acceptable providing that a hole is cut in the garment to accommodate the stoma. The roll-on should be put on, and the exact site of the stoma marked on the fabric, then a hole should be cut large enough for the bag to be brought through. The raw edges of the hole can be blanket stitched or bound with soft bias binding. It is advisable to use an easy-fitting roll-on, as care must be taken to avoid undue constriction post-operatively. Ultimately, a specially made stoma girdle can be fitted by a trained surgical appliance fitter, if it is considered to be necessary and the patient desires it.

Tights are on sale in large stores which are made in separate legs. These are very useful for ostomists, as there is no crotch gusset or seam.

Any preferred style of clothes may be worn, and the modern light-weight bags are quite undetectable and rustle-free.

For swimming or sunbathing most women find a one-piece swimsuit comfortable. A two-piece costume with the bottom half cut to reach the waistline can also be worn without discomfort or self-consciousness.

CORRECT USE OF SKIN PROTECTIVES

The advantages and suitability of the various products and techniques for skin protection should be assessed on the individual needs of each patient. Some methods in current use are outlined below:

1) *Barrier creams* – all cream should be used sparingly and massaged well into the skin. All trace of greasiness must be wiped away before fitting a new adhesive appliance. Creams are not suitable for sore or broken skin.

2) *Skin gels* – these usually dry quickly and do not leave a greasy surface. The minimum amount to cover the area thinly should be used, but should never be applied to a sore or excoriated skin.

3) *Medical adhesive sprays* – these must only be used to spray on to a double-sided plaster, or the face-plate of an appliance – never on to the body directly. Great care, and a special adhesive remover, needs to be used in conjunction with these products to avoid trauma to the skin.

4) *Stomahesive wafer* – it is essential that the stoma is measured and that the hole in the Stomahesive is a close fit around the stoma, to eliminate the risk of leakage on to the peristomal skin. Accurate fitting of the Stomahesive is particularly vital where the effluent is liquid or semi-liquid. Stomahesive may be used over skin that is sore and broken.

5) *Karaya rings and 'blankets'* – these products are soft and flexible and may be used to mould round a stoma to act as a protective barrier.

6) *Karaya paste* – may be used to fill in small gulleys and depressions near to the stoma. Apply to sound skin areas only.

7) *Karaya powder* – will adhere to broken areas of skin and offer some protection.

With improved standards of stoma care there is a noticeable decrease in the incidence of serious skin problems related to stoma management. However, steps must be taken immediately to remedy any slight reddening or soreness of the skin, and there is an extensive range of skin care accessories available for use by every ostomist.

QUESTIONS FOR DISCUSSION

1) What are the advantages to be gained by pre-operative siting of a stoma on: a) an obese patient? b) an emaciated patient?
   Mention all the general factors to be considered when siting a stoma before operation.

2) What do you consider to be the main considerations in the routine care of a stoma patient on the ward?

3) What advice on changing his own appliance would you give to a stoma patient: a) in hospital? b) at home?

4) Describe an acceptable method of disposal of soiled appliances: a) in hospital, b) at home, c) on holiday.

5) Discuss methods of combating odour.

6) What advice on clothes would you give to both male and female ostomists? Is it necessary to have special clothing?

7) Detail the skin protective agents available and their correct usage.

Chapter 5

Specific Aspects of Ileostomy Care

TYPE OF EFFLUENT

A patient with an ileostomy normally loses from 500 to 850ml of effluent in 24 hours. The consistency is often described as being similar to porridge, and is paler in colour than the formed faeces from the large bowel. The discharge will be copious and watery in the immediate post-operative period, when the loss may be as high as 1000 to 1500ml in a day. Careful monitoring of the intake and output of fluids must be maintained, and immediate action taken to remedy any fluid deficiency or electrolyte imbalance caused by an excessive discharge from the stoma (see Chapter 15, 'Changes in Stomal Action', page 195).

Most ileostomy patients find it necessary to empty their appliances three or four times a day, and immediately before retiring for the night, though the volume of effluent and frequency of stomal action will vary from person to person.

SKIN CARE AIDS

Ileal effluent contains enzymes which will 'digest' and excoriate the surrounding layers of epidermis if allowed to leak and settle on the skin around the stoma. As soon as there is any sign of leakage, however slight, the appliance should be removed and the skin washed carefully with warm water and a mild soap before fitting a clean appliance.

There is a comprehensive range of skin care accessories available on prescription. A barrier cream, skin gel or protective spray should be used routinely on a sound skin before the fitting of any type of adhesive appliance (see Chapter 4, 'Correct Use of Skin Protectives', page 67).

If a person is known to have a sensitive skin, or if the skin has become sore, a substance such as Stomahesive or karaya must be used

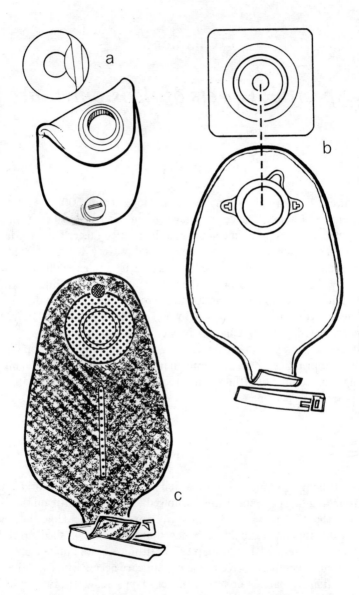

Figure 5.1 Ileostomy appliances. a) Rubber bag with separate flange, double-sided plaster. Screw outlet. b) Stomahesive flange with separate clip-on bag. Clip closure. Two sizes. c) Coloured bag with flatus filter and clear view panel. Clip closure.

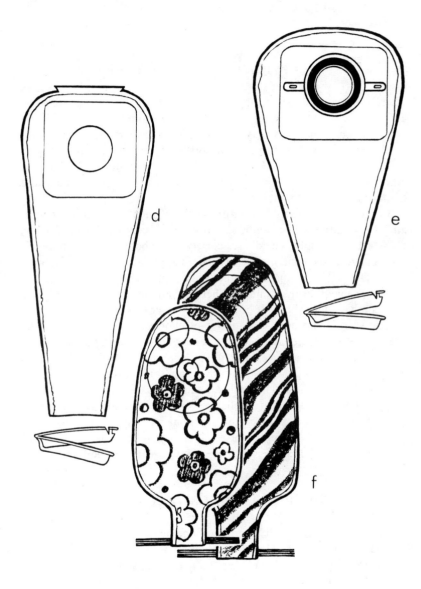

Figure 5.1 Ileostomy appliances (continued). d) Adhesive flexible flange. Clip closure. e) Karaya ring with micropore adhesive flange. Integral belt fitments. Clip closure. f) Coloured patterned bags. Two sizes. Integral wind-up wire closure.

to cover the area affected at all times before an adhesive appliance is fitted.

TYPES OF APPLIANCE

There are many ranges of appliances available, both in the one-piece and two-piece styles (see Figure 5.1). All ileostomy appliances should be drainable so that they may be emptied as necessary, and can remain in place for three to seven days according to circumstances and personal preference. It is desirable to avoid constant removal of an adhesive ileostomy appliance, to minimise the risk of soreness and damage to the peristomal skin.

Because of the semi-solid nature of the effluent from an ileostomy, and the potential danger to the skin if leakage occurs, it is vital that the chosen style of appliance adheres closely to the body, with no space left for seepage of the contents. Most modern appliances are manufactured from odour resistant material, and unpleasant odour is not normally a serious problem for ileostomists. There are a number of preparations to help combat odour should it occur (see Chapter 4, 'Odour', page 65).

The size of bag used is a matter of choice. Most ileostomists will prefer a bag which enables them to enjoy a convenient period of time between emptying, and a good night's sleep undisturbed by the fear of an overflowing appliance. Mini size bags are available for special occasions, or for those who prefer a smaller shape. Cotton bag covers are obtainable to fit most appliances or can be made very easily at home from odd scraps of cotton material. A bag cover is useful to prevent the plastic or rubber of an appliance from constantly coming into contact with the skin, and causing soreness and discomfort.

'CONTROL' OF ILEOSTOMY ACTION

Ileostomy action cannot be controlled, and no new ileostomist should be misled on this point. However, the ileostomy will be most active approximately half an hour after the main meals of the day, and less active at other times. It is extremely inadvisable, and inherently harmful, to attempt to limit the amount of effluent by curtailing the intake of food and drink. Ileostomists require a routinely high intake of fluids to stabilise their water balance, and the volume of the effluent is related to the diet taken and not to the quantity of fluid drunk.

Ileostomy dysfunction can occur, and may take the form of obstruction, often due to a bolus of insufficiently masticated food, mechanical complications related to the structure and condition of the stoma itself. It may also take the form of an abnormally high effluent output, which could lead to metabolic disturbance (see Chapters 12, 13 and 15).

SEX AND THE ILEOSTOMIST

The conditions for which ileostomy is performed occur normally in a younger age group, and consideration must be given to the possibility of some degree of sexual dysfunction after surgery. These difficulties are often temporary, and lessen or disappear when the general health is greatly improved, which happily often occurs with this group of ostomists.

In all cases, it is wise for each patient to discuss any problems or queries with his or her own doctor. The stoma care nurse is also ready to give all the help and information that she can to solve specific dilemmas, and many patients find comfort and reassurance in 'talking out' their troubles with a sympathetic third party. Help may be requested by teenage or young adult ileostomists who are unsure of how or when to explain their stoma to girl or boyfriends, or who need confirmation that they are potentially suitable marriage partners. It has been said that sex is 95 per cent mental and 5 per cent physical, so that the psychological factor is very strong and may cause physical malfunction (see Chapter 1).

SPECIFIC DIFFICULTIES OF THE MALE

Male potency can be affected by ostomy surgery, because of interference with the nerves which control the sexual functions of the genitalia. Failure to achieve or maintain an erection is a common problem immediately post-operatively, but in many cases the disability is temporary. It is important for the male and female to realise that a full recovery from surgery and a build up of general health is advisable before attempting normal sexual activity. Patience is the key word for both partners.

SPECIFIC DIFFICULTIES OF THE FEMALE

Soreness of the perineal area may persist for some months after surgery, and normal sexual intercourse should be delayed until the perineal incision has healed firmly. Intercourse may be slightly uncomfortable at first, due to the scarring from the incision, but this should wear off in time. Persistent pain should be reported to the surgeon in charge of the case for an investigation to be made into the cause.

HELPFUL SUGGESTIONS

Confidence and pleasure in love-making can be achieved if care is taken to ensure that there is no fear of leakage or odour. Scrupulous cleanliness, great care in securing and emptying the bag and the wearing of opaque, odour-free plastic adhesive appliances should avoid these problems. For the male, the appliance can be concealed by a cloth bag cover, a cummerbund under which the bag may be securely tucked, or by the wearing of smart boxer style shorts. Ladies have many options for the concealment of their appliances, and can make sure that they wear the smallest and neatest bag that is practical. Appliance covers can be made from any pretty material, perhaps to match a frilly nightie, or matching crotch-less panties may be worn.

In the interest of romance, the ostomist would be well advised to avoid eating or drinking anything which might cause excessive flatus, or some other upset, during intimacy.

If it is felt by either partner that the stoma or the appliance seems to get in the way during intercourse, then different positions should be tried. Very often this type of loving experimentation results in greatly enhanced mutual pleasure and sexual satisfaction.

CONTRACEPTION

Oral contraceptives are taken by a great number of female ileostomists, and there is no evidence that unwanted pregnancies have resulted from malabsorption of the Pill. The extra risk of thromboembolism may exclude the Pill in cases of Crohn's disease. Further discussion of this subject may be found in Chapter 13. Another reliable method of contraception would be a properly fitted intra-uterine device, although this is something which should be discussed with the doctor, and the coil fitted by him.

PREGNANCY

It is recommended that two years are allowed to elapse before pregnancy is considered, to permit perineal healing, and most women are advised to limit themselves to producing two babies. However, there are many exceptions to this rule, and frank discussion with the doctor before attempting to conceive would be the wisest course to take.

The first problem in pregnancy is to conceive. In general, an uncomplicated pregnancy can be expected once conception has occurred. Problems such as displacement, enlargement, prolapse or retraction of the stoma may occur, but usually resolve themselves as soon as the birth is over.

With increasing girth, the most common management problem is the impossibility of actually seeing the stoma when trying to effect an appliance change, but a judicious arrangement of mirrors, or a little help from a spouse, will make things easier, and most pregnant ileostomists evolve their own personal system to overcome this difficulty.

Anaemia is a possible condition in early pregnancy, particularly where an intolerance to oral iron is present, and an alternative method of administration might be needed. The most serious complication of pregnancy in ostomists is that of intestinal obstruction, and immediate hospital treatment is indicated if this should occur. Sometimes it is difficult to differentiate between the onset of labour pains and intestinal colic, and this may lead to a potentially dangerous delay in diagnosis and treatment. Any severe abdominal pain must be reported at once to the doctor for his assessment.

All pregnant ileostomists should be delivered of their babies in hospital, and in the majority of cases normal vaginal delivery is both possible and desirable. The ileostomy itself is rarely a cause for delivery by Caesarian section, though there may be obstetrical reasons for Caesarian intervention. Where an episiotomy incision is necessary to facilitate vaginal delivery it will be made so as to avoid the existing perineal scar.

Breast feeding the baby is possible if the mother so desires, providing that the previous surgery has not caused problems of intestinal malabsorption.

Whether to have a baby or not is a private and personal decision, and there are many happy mothers of healthy babies who also have an ileostomy to care for. Their success is an encouragement and reassurance to other ileostomists.

REFERENCES

Nash, Ellison D. F. 1976. *Principles and Practice of Surgery for Nurses and Allied Professions* 6th edition. Edward Arnold.

Gibson, John (ed.) 1975. *Modern Medicine for Nurses* 3rd edition. Blackwell Scientific Publications.

QUESTIONS FOR DISCUSSION

1) What is the effect of leakage of effluent from an ileostomy on to the skin? What steps would you take to ensure that the skin was protected?

2) What would be a suitable type of appliance for a patient with an ileostomy to use?

3) Why is it important for ileostomists to take extra fluids? What would be the effect of an insufficient fluid intake?

4) Discuss possible sexual difficulties of the male ileostomist.

5) Are there any specific problems which may occur if an ileostomist becomes pregnant?

Chapter 6

Specific Aspects of Colostomy Care

TYPE OF EFFLUENT

Ascending colostomy – the discharge from a stoma sited in the ascending colon will be semi-liquid and flow almost continuously.

Transverse colostomy – the discharge from a stoma sited in the transverse colon is semi-liquid to semi-solid and the action is frequent and copious.

Caecostomy – the discharge from an opening made into the caecum is liquid and frequent.

Sigmoid colostomy – the discharge from a stoma sited in the descending or sigmoid colon is a formed, solid stool which often settles down to a movement once or twice a day. (See Figure 6.1.)

'CONTROL' OF COLOSTOMY ACTION

Irrigation of the colon per stoma is practised widely in some countries as a means of regulating the emptying of bowel contents at a fixed time (see Chapter 11).

The discharge of faeces per stoma is involuntary and not controllable by sphincter action, so that it is misleading and untrue to assure patients that eventually they will only have one action a day at a time most convenient to them.

In the case of a stoma sited in the ascending or transverse colon, where the effluent is semi-fluid and almost continuous, the patient can have no control over evacuation other than to avoid the sort of diet which will cause excessive flatus, odour or diarrhoea (see Chapter 12 on Diet).

Many patients with permanent sigmoid colostomies are able to manipulate their diet and meal times so as to achieve a relatively regular pattern of bowel movement. The ease with which modern stoma

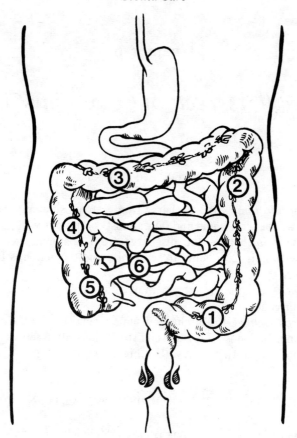

Figure 6.1   Types of stoma and typical sites.

Stoma	Colon removed or by-passed	Type of effluent
1. Sigmoid colostomy	Part of sigmoid colon and whole of rectum	Firm, solid, separate stool
2. Descending colostomy	Descending colon below splenic flexure and whole of rectum	Formed stool
3. Transverse colostomy, doubled-barrelled or loop	All of the colon and rectum distal to the stoma	Semi-liquid
4. Ascending colostomy	All of the colon and rectum distal to the stoma	Semi-liquid
5. Caecostomy	All of the colon and rectum distal to the stoma	Liquid
6. Ileostomy	Usually the entire colon and rectum	Liquid and continuous

bags can be changed, at any time and in any private place, is a form of control acceptable to very many colostomists.

Control is an inaccurate word to use in connection with faecal evacuation per stoma – good management would be a better phrase.

SKIN CARE

Care must always be taken to protect the skin around a stoma from soreness or damage, and the needs vary with the type of effluent and the frequency of stomal action. Frequent liquid or semi-liquid faecal discharge, which may contain harmful enzymes, will require special attention to ensure that no potentially harmful matter is allowed to reach and remain on the peristomal skin. The skin must also be protected from the damaging effects resulting from repeated application and removal of adhesive appliances.

The correct use of skin protective agents currently available to ostomy patients is discussed fully in Chapter 4, 'Correct Use of Skin Protectives' (page 67), and it cannot be stressed too often that care of the skin around the stoma is of the utmost importance. Any negligence will lead to unnecessary distress and discomfort.

TYPES OF APPLIANCE

The type of appliance chosen will obviously depend upon the stoma itself, the amount of normal output and the most convenient and comfortable style of bag to contain that output. The choice of appliance is also influenced by the nature of the effluent and the need to ensure maximum resistance to unpleasant odour. Examples of different colostomy appliances are shown in Figure 6.2.

Flatus can pose a real problem. As already mentioned, most of the newer types of appliance incorporate a flatus release filter with a charcoal layer to deodorise the gas. There are also separate filter patches which may be stuck over pinprick holes made near the top of the bag.

Drainable bags can be deflated by opening the bottom outlet, though there is no reason why flatus filter patches should not be used on the top part of this type of appliance also. Care has to be taken to ensure that there is no leakage of bag contents through too large flatus release holes, and sometimes the filters themselves can become blocked.

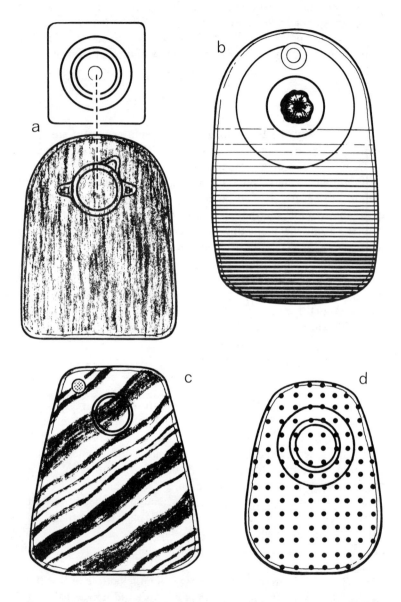

Figure 6.2 Colostomy appliances. a) Stomahesive flange with opaque closed clip-on bag. b) Coloured lightweight bag with flexible adhesive flange. c) Adhesive patterned bag with flatus filter. d) Mini size patterned bag.

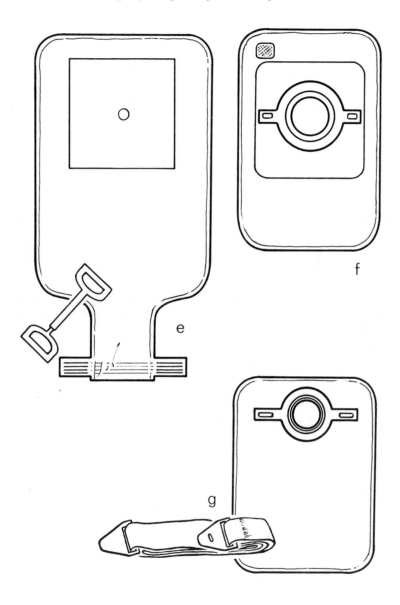

Figure 6.2 Colostomy appliances (continued). e) Drainable post-operative bag. Large flexible karaya flange. Integral wind-up closure. f) Microporous adhesive flange with belt tags and flatus filter in bag. g) Non-adhesive bag worn with a belt.

With two-piece appliances it is simple to release flatus by detaching the top of the bag from the flange, but a deodorant air spray should be used before doing so wherever possible. Many patients like to instil a few drops of deodorant into the bag as it cuts down the odour on emptying.

Most established ostomists realise which foods or drinks produce the most flatus, and take steps to avoid them.

Ascending colostomy

The effluent is semi-fluid and continuous, and will contain harmful digestive juices, so that a drainable adhesive bag, either one-piece or two-piece, with the routine use of an efficient skin protection barrier such as Stomahesive, must be fitted. Non-adhesive appliances are not suitable.

Transverse colostomy

The effluent is normally semi-liquid and copious, and the stoma, either double-barrelled or loop, is likely to be very big and awkwardly sited. A large drainable appliance is required, and those fitted with a flexible karaya face-plate and generous size of attached bag are useful and comfortable. This type of appliance can be fitted closely round the stoma, and on top of any kind of ostomy bridge which may have been inserted to support the loop. Other types of large, drainable adhesive bags may be used, but a protective Stomahesive wafer must be placed underneath to protect the skin from excoriation due to leakage. Non-adhesive appliances are not suitable.

Sigmoid colostomy

An adhesive drainable appliance with skin protection underneath will be required in the immediate post-operative period. When normal intestinal activity is resumed, and the stool becomes formed, there is a wide variety of closed bags, with or without an adhesive flange, from which to choose. It is advisable to provide the patient with both drainable and closed bags on discharge from hospital in order to cope with any episodes of loose stool which might occur. Some method of deodorised flatus release is desirable, and attention must be paid to the preservation of the peristomal skin.

If a more or less regular pattern of bowel movement is attained it is possible for some ostomists to wear a small stoma cap or mini pouch for certain activities without fear of embarrassment, for example for sports or during sexual intercourse.

Appliances for the permanent sigmoid colostomy may be one-piece or two-piece, coloured, patterned and plain, adhesive or non-adhesive, and are mostly fashioned from odour-free and rustle-free plastic. Cotton covers are available for use, particularly in hot weather, and many patients make their own from odd scraps of cotton material.

CARE OF THE LOOP COLOSTOMY

The function of the *loop* or defunctioning colostomy is to divert the faecal stream to the outside, thus by-passing any trauma, disease or surgery to the left colon or the rectum (see Figure 6.3).

Some means of supporting the loop of bowel on the body surface has to be used, and there are several different types available to the surgeon. It is necessary to discourage spillage of faecal matter from the proximal to the defunctioning distal loop, though this is not always perfectly achieved. Such means of support include:

1) Glass rods of varying length, with soft rubber tubing attached to each end after insertion through the loop of gut, which have been widely used for years. However, they are unwieldy and very difficult to accommodate within an appliance.

2) Short length of soft rubber tubing inserted through the loop and sutured to the abdominal surface at each end.

3) Plastic rods inserted subcutaneously.

4) Plastic bridges of varying shapes, for example wishbone design or double-ended key shape, are now used extensively. These are both easier to insert and remove, more comfortable for the patient, and much less difficult to manage for the nurse.

5) Sometimes the antimesenteric surfaces of the loop of bowel are sutured together for 10cm to form a spur under the exteriorised top of the loop. The spur is subsequently crushed by enterotome to close the colostomy.

Normally a rod or bridge will be left in situ for 5 to 10 days, but the surgeon's directions must always be followed with regard to the removal of the loop support. Problems can arise in the management of a patient with a loop colostomy and the stoma should be carefully observed for any adverse signs.

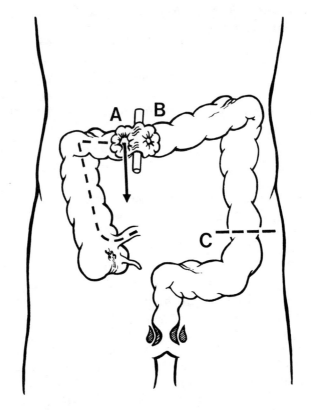

Figure 6.3 Temporary loop colostomy with rod in situ.
a) Proximal opening. b) Distal opening. c) Anastamosis site.

SURGICAL PROBLEMS

Retraction – a loop colostomy, particularly in an obese person, may retract after the supporting rod is removed.

Prolapse – more commonly the distal limb of a transverse colostomy may prolapse to a considerable length, but it can also occur with the proximal end. Gross prolapse of the stoma makes it very difficult to fit into an appliance comfortably.

Strangulation – occasionally strangulation may follow prolapse and reconstruction of the stoma may be necessary.

Ischaemia – if the blood supply to the stoma is impaired and it becomes ischaemic, refashioning will be required.

All the above conditions require the attention of the surgeon and must be reported immediately.

PROBLEMS OF MANAGEMENT

Loop colostomies are usually fashioned in the right transverse colon, as an emergency procedure, and the stoma is, therefore, not sited pre-operatively. These stomas are often brought out high under the rib cage, are large in size, and discharge semi-liquid faeces almost continuously (see section on siting, between pages 190 and 191).

Secure and comfortable fitting of a large size bag can be difficult due to awkward siting of a bulky stoma, plus supporting rod or bridge. Modern flexible flange adhesive drainable appliances which can be cut to fit the stoma very accurately make this problem easier to solve.

Spillage of faeces from the proximal to the distal loop may occur, and there may be considerable faecal residue in the defunctioned section of bowel. The passing of faecal matter per rectum after loop colostomy is perfectly normal and the patient should be warned that this may happen. The patient should also be told that it is to be expected that there will be a certain amount of mucous discharge per rectum, and that this is not a cause for alarm.

PREPARATION FOR CLOSURE OF COLOSTOMY

A temporary colostomy is closed as soon as possible after the primary cause for which it was raised has been dealt with by further surgery. A careful check of the soundness of the surgery is undertaken before closure is attempted. These pre-operative procedures include:
1) Distal (defunctioning) loop washouts, prior to –
2) Barium enema and X-ray to assess the anastamosis and patency of the bowel;
3) Distal loop washouts to clear the barium from the defunctioned segment;
4) The administration of aperients and antibiotics by mouth to prepare the *proximal* bowel;
5) Pre-operative reduction of solid diet;
6) Pre-operative distal colon washout with warm water or saline. Neomycin sulphate is sometimes used.
N.B. It is useless to administer *oral* aperients in an attempt to clear the distal loop.

SEX AND THE COLOSTOMIST

Due to the fact that most colostomy operations are performed on persons over 40 years of age, the sexual problems of this group tend to be related to age, existing physical infirmities and the extent of the relevant surgery.

Individual discussion of sexual problems with doctor or surgeon is advisable.

MALE DYSFUNCTION

Some degree of impotence is suffered by a relatively high proportion of male colostomists after rectal surgery, due to damage to the system of nerves serving the genitalia. Many of the men who can achieve erection and orgasm cannot ejaculate, and the seminal fluid is propelled backwards into the bladder (retrograde ejaculation). Other men are unable to maintain an erection or reach orgasm.

FEMALE DYSFUNCTION

Women do not suffer the same impairment of sexual achievement, but many complain of dryness and pain during intercourse, particularly where the upper third of the vaginal wall has been removed during the operation. An excess of scar tissue may cause vaginal stricture. Stress urinary incontinence can be a problem, but avoidance of fluids for some time before coitus and an empty bladder should prevent embarrassment during love-making.

CONTRACEPTION

A large proportion of female colostomists are over child-bearing age, or have no desire for more children, but there is no contra-indication to taking the Pill and no problem of malabsorption.

An intra-uterine device is not usually advised for female colostomists due to the frequent involvement of the vagina in the rectal surgery, and to the higher incidence of pelvic sepsis with the use of this means of contraception.

PREGNANCY

There is no reason why colostomists should not conceive and have a successful pregnancy. The fact that they belong generally to an older age group may cause some problems of pregnancy unrelated to the fact that stoma surgery has been performed (see Chapter 5, 'Pregnancy and the Ileostomist', page 75).

A caring, sharing relationship, with each partner willing to accept the limitations of the other is the best and most successful format for the continuation of a mutually rewarding sex-life after surgery. This is something that has to be worked out between the two people concerned. Help and expert advice are available and may contribute towards solving some of the difficulties (see also Chapters 8, 16 and 17). The majority of ostomists eventually find their own solutions.

QUESTIONS FOR DISCUSSION

1) What would be a suitable type of appliance for: a) an ascending colostomy? b) a loop colostomy? c) a sigmoid colostomy.

2) Mention the means by which a loop colostomy may be supported on the abdominal surface.

3) What steps would you take to prepare a patient for closure of a temporary colostomy?

4) Discuss possible sexual difficulties of the male colostomist.

5) Are there any specific difficulties which may occur if a patient with a colostomy becomes pregnant?

Chapter 7

Everyday Lifestyle Management and Information for the Ostomist

One of the main worries for the majority of patients, both before and after surgery, is wondering whether their accustomed style of living will be radically altered by the acquisition of a stoma. Some adjustments will obviously need to be considered post-operatively; but informed and commonsense support from doctors, nurses, other caring services, and their own family members, will assist each individual to reach a personally satisfying level of success in coming to terms with everyday life as an ostomist.

WORK

The timing of a return to work after surgery depends more upon general health than upon the fact that the person now has a stoma. Whatever the type of job, it is important that toilet facilities are available, and that privacy is assured for changing or emptying the appliance. If difficulties arise over the provision of these facilities, an approach can be made to the employer by a social worker, possibly with the help of the family doctor and stoma care nurse concerned. Most employers are found to be co-operative and understanding once the reasons have been explained to them.

Strenuous manual work, or a job which entails heavy lifting or digging, is unsuitable following extensive abdominal surgery. It is recommended that the advice of the Disablement Resettlement Officer is sought over the question of a change of employment or retraining for a different occupation. The DRO may be contacted through the local Job Centre or the Department of Health and Social Security office.

RECREATIONAL ACTIVITIES

There is no reason why the greater number of ostomists should not be able to return to most of the recreational pursuits which they enjoyed before surgery, though this ability would be governed by their physical state and degree of motivation. All patients should be reassured that there is every possibility that they can take up their favourite hobby or sport again as soon as they feel well enough to do so.

Swimming is an excellent sport enjoyed by ostomists of all ages. It is essential that the stoma is covered during swimming, either by continuing to wear the usual bag or by using a smaller waterproof bag or stoma cap. These small bags would be completely undetectable under swimwear and contain any effluent for the requisite length of time. For added security, four strips of waterproof strapping may be used to seal the edges of the bag or patch.

For sports like cricket, tennis and football, where damage to the stoma might occur, some appliances incorporate a rigid protective bridge over the stoma, thus guarding it from injury. A broad supportive belt or girdle may be worn, with a cushioning pad over the stoma appliance, whenever vigorous bodily contact is likely to be a part of the sporting activity, or if something like rock climbing is contemplated.

Pursuits such as dancing, riding and cycling are all possible, together with less strenuous pastimes like bowls or gardening. These days, people with a stoma can do most of the things which they themselves feel able to attempt, though commonsense should always prevail and any necessary precautions be taken to avoid injury or accident.

HOLIDAYS

Many people with stomas feel that they are now precluded from going away for a holiday, either at home or abroad, and need a lot of advice and reassurance before taking the plunge. Providing certain commonsense rules are followed, and an adequate supply of all necessary items packed, no insurmountable problems should be encountered (see Chapter 4, 'Disposal away from Home', page 65).

When travelling away from home it is essential to pack a good supply of bags and accessories in the hand luggage so that all the materials for stoma care are readily accessible during the journey (see 'Travel Kit', page 91).

Flatus

It is sometimes found that travel by air causes an excess of flatus. To help counteract this effect, it would be wise to wear an appliance with an attached flatus filter, and to take care not to eat or drink wind-producing substances.

Storage

Storage of bags in a hot climate can be difficult, and there are many different ways discovered by ostomists to minimise the damage caused by an excessively hot or humid environment. These expedients include storing the appliances in a net suspended below a roof fan in Egypt; keeping them in a refrigerated picnic box in Mauritius; between layers of foil on a marble slab in Abu Dhabi; and in a water-cooled meat safe in Haifa.

It is not recommended that rubber or plastic appliances, Stomahesive or karaya products, are kept permanently in a refrigerator, as this will impair their efficiency by causing brittleness and structural deterioration. The coolest, driest and best ventilated cupboard, drawer, or other container, is the place of choice for storage of ostomy supplies in hot countries. The storage unit itself should be placed away from any source of direct heat or sunlight.

Diet

Anyone can get a 'Gyppy tummy' on holiday in another country, and ostomists are no exception. Extra care should be taken with strange food and drink, and it is worth remembering that the tap water in some countries is not safe to drink unboiled. An intake of extra fluids is vital for ostomists in hot climates, in view of the amount lost due to excessive sweating, otherwise dehydration and electrolyte imbalance may occur.

Highly spiced and exotic foods should be approached with caution and a sudden increase in alcohol consumption may also cause quite a few problems (see Chapter 12, 'Diet').

Medication

Wise travellers take with them all the medications they might need whilst away from home, as it is both difficult and embarrassing to mime 'diarrhoea', for example, to a foreign pharmacist who speaks no English. Drugs and medical advice are sometimes difficult to obtain when on holiday and are also very expensive, so that it is much better to travel equipped to deal with simple upsets should they occur (see Chapter 13 on 'Medication').

STORAGE OF APPLIANCES

Appliances should *not* be stored:
1) In the bathroom, because it is likely to get hot and steamy;
2) On a sunny window-sill;
3) On a shelf or in a cupboard over a radiator or fire;
4) Close to any other source of heat;
5) In a refrigerator or freezer;
6) In a damp situation, as, for example under the kitchen sink.

Appliances *should* be stored in a cool, dry and airy place away from direct sunlight and extremes of temperature. They should be used in strict rotation so that none is kept for an excessively long period, which might cause a deterioration in quality.

CHANGE KIT

It is advisable to have a 'change kit' always prepared so that an appliance change can be effected with the minimum amount of time and trouble whenever necessary. A lidded box containing already prepared appliances, cut to size and ready for fitting, plus any special creams, deodorants or skin protectives and a supply of tissues or swabs can be kept conveniently at hand for use at any time, and should be replenished as required from the main stocks. Adhesive tape and a small pair of scissors should also be a part of the 'change kit', together with a stoma size guide and a mirror (if used). An appliance change can be done very quickly and simply if all the requirements are kept together in this way.

TRAVEL KIT

All people with a stoma need to carry a 'travel kit' in jacket pocket or handbag, so that an emergency appliance change can be managed when out of reach of home facilities.

A typical 'travel kit' could include:
1) Prepared clean appliance;
2) Folded soft tissues;
3) Small phial of cleansing lotion or impregnated 'wipe' – for use when water is unavailable;
4) Folded empty plastic bag and wire closure – for the soiled appliance, if immediate disposal is impossible;
5) Small spray deodorant;

6) Small pair of scissors.

Personal preference will suggest additions to, and omissions from, the contents of a 'travel kit', but the aim must be to have all the basics for a change of appliance available, without having to carry a bulky or obtrusive package.

EQUIPMENT

After discharge from hospital, an ostomist needs to be in possession of clear and detailed written information regarding the equipment required for stoma care and exactly how to obtain it. A card containing precise details of all necessities must be prepared and given to the patient before leaving the ward, accompanied by at least two weeks' supply of appropriate appliances and skin aids.

The information card should note:

1) Make, size and type of appliance – including the order number, quantity and head office address of the manufacturer or supplier.
2) Details of any skin care aids, special lotions or deodorants being used. The correct name, order number and quantity required should be stated.
3) Any other accessories required, for example strapping, belts, closure clips, dressings. The correct name, order number and quantity required should be given.

PRESCRIPTIONS

A prescription form FP.10 must be obtained from the patient's own family doctor listing equipment requirements as detailed on the information card. This prescription may be taken to a retail pharmacist, sent to a supply company, or by direct pre-paid mail to those appliance companies who operate a customer service. Some patients are able to have their supplies dispensed from a Group Practice Health Centre. In all cases a doctor's prescription is required, the appropriate exemption box on the back of the form must be ticked, and the form signed and dated. It is usual to prescribe quantities for one month, to avoid stock-piling and storage problems in the home, but extra supplies may be prescribed in special circumstances. A repeat prescription should be ordered in the third week of the month as there may well be a delay in the delivery of supplies, and there must always be an overlap to avoid running out of essentials.

It is advisable to take adequate supplies of stoma care equipment when going away from home as it can be awkward to obtain a prescription from an unfamiliar doctor, and impossible to obtain the necessary items quickly from a chemist in a strange town. Similarly, it is wise for ostomists entering hospital to take in a supply of their own appliances, as not all hospitals are stocked with a wide variety of stoma equipment.

EXEMPTION CERTIFICATES

Exemption from prescription charges is available to patients with permanent stomas. Males under 65 years and females under 60 years should obtain a Prescription Exemption Form FC.91/EC.91, which will entitle them to receive all prescribable items free of charge. These forms are obtainable on demand from main Post Offices, or may often be supplied with the information card by the stoma care nurse before the patient is discharged home. Exemption certificates are valid for a period of 5 years, after which application for renewal must be made to the local Family Practitioners Committee. Only stoma needs are met without charge, and the appliances requested must be those which are accepted as prescribable on a Prescription Form FP.10.

Every stoma patient is an individual who requires the type of care suited to his own particular needs, and the age group to which he belongs. Older patients, perhaps with impaired sight or arthritic hands, may find it too difficult to manage the more complicated bags and must be helped to find a simpler system (see Chapter 16, 'Lifestyle Problems').

Personal preference must be balanced by proper dietary management and correct medication (see Chapters 12 and 13).

Frank discussion of sexual difficulties with someone qualified to give informed and sympathetic advice will often help towards solving some of the intimate problems (see Chapters 1, 5 and 6).

Patients with bowel stomas, temporary or permanent, require expert nursing care and management. A comprehensive knowledge of suitable appliances and skin protectives, plus an understanding of psychological needs and difficulties, will all contribute to an improved standard of care for ostomists.

REFERENCES

Crown, Sidney 1976. *Psychosexual Problems*. Academic Press.
Ellis, Harold and Wastell, Christopher (eds) 1976. *General Surgery for Nurses*. Blackwell Scientific Publications.

QUESTIONS FOR DISCUSSION

1) Discuss the factors to be considered before an ostomist returns to work after surgery.
2) Detail the difficulties which may be encountered by ostomists travelling away from home. Suggest solutions to the problems of stoma care in a hot climate.
3) Where should stoma equipment *not* be stored? Give reasons.
4) Why should ostomists carry the necessities for an appliance change with them at all times? What should this 'travel kit' contain?
5) Detail the information and equipment which should be given to every stoma patient before discharge from hospital.

Chapter 8

Urinary Stomas and their Management

The outlook for patients requiring urinary diversion has improved significantly over the last few years. This is partly due to advances in surgical technique, but also to the appointment of specially trained stoma care nurses and to the advent of the lightweight disposable appliance.

Patients are no longer expected to cope alone with leakage problems, skin excoriation and bulky non-disposable equipment. Stoma care begins before the operation when adequate psychological preparation, as well as physical preparation, helps the patient to accept the concept of a new and unexpected body image.

Following the operation, the patient must be taught to manage his stoma and appliance, so that by the time of discharge he is confident and independent of others. Regular visits to the Stoma Clinic, and help from an experienced community nurse, rapidly establishes confidence and independence.

Close follow-up of every patient by stoma care nurses following urinary diversion has helped to create high standards of care, and to provide the early detection and correction of long term problems associated with this type of specialised surgery.

Urine, being fluid, must be collected in a watertight apparatus which adheres to the body, preventing leakage and skin excoriation. Urinary stomas should protrude from the surface of the skin by at least 2cm, so that the urine is conveyed directly into the collecting apparatus. Careful planning of the site for the stoma, and a scrupulous surgical technique, are vitally important in the prevention of many long term problems.

INDICATIONS FOR URINARY DIVERSION

MALIGNANCY

The commonest cause for urinary diversion is locally advanced carcinoma of the bladder, often treated by total cystectomy with preoperative radiotherapy. On other occasions, radical radiotherapy is the treatment of choice and cystectomy is only performed if the cancer recurs.

Tumours of the urethra are difficult to manage and usually require cystectomy.

In women, carcinoma of the cervix or uterus may invade the bladder, and require a cystectomy in addition to radical hysterectomy.

Palliative diversion of the urine for untreatable pelvic cancer is seldom indicated. These patients usually develop obstructive uraemia, which should be left undisturbed.

URINARY FISTULAE

Carcinoma of the cervix is often treated by high dose local radiotherapy. In some patients this may lead to extensive fibrosis of normal pelvic tissue, with the late development of vesico-vaginal or recto-vaginal fistulae. Attempts at local repair are futile and urinary or faecal diversion are necessary.

Ectopia vesicae is a congenital abnormality of the bladder, resulting in malformation of the anterior bladder wall. This can be thought of as a large anterior bladder fistula.

Severe epispadias in either sex results in failure of the anterior walls of the urethra to unite.

UNMANAGEABLE INCONTINENCE

The normal life of many patients can be severely affected as a result of urinary incontinence. In men, this can usually be managed by some form of external incontinence device. The latter are unsuitable for women, most of whom would prefer urinary diversion to permanent incontinence. The usual causes of such incontinence in women are multiple sclerosis, spina bifida and other neurological abnormalities; stress incontinence with bladder stability for which numerous operations have failed, interstitial cystitis, treated tuberculosis of the bladder, and traumatic paraplegia.

METHODS OF URINARY DIVERSION

There are several ways in which to divert the flow of urine, and it is important to consider each patient individually before deciding upon the best method to choose. An elderly patient with failing eyesight or arthritic fingers may not be able to manage an external collecting apparatus successfully, and uretero-colic diversion would be preferable. A patient with multiple sclerosis will not be able to control a rectal bladder due to an incompetent anal sphincter, and is best served by an ileal conduit.

URETEROSIGMOIDOSTOMY

For many years implantation of the ureters into the sigmoid colon has been a popular and successful method of urinary diversion. However, long term problems associated with the reabsorption of electrolytes, ascending infection, pyelonephritis and renal failure have led many surgeons to select alternative methods.

ILEAL CONDUIT

The ileal conduit, originally described by Eugene Bricker in 1950 and known as the Bricker Loop, has proved to be the most popular and successful method of permanent urinary diversion. Often incorrectly referred to as an ileal bladder, the Bricker Loop is not intended to replace the bladder and act as a reservoir for urine, but is simply a means of conveying urine from the ureters to the surface of the skin, where an external appliance acts as the reservoir.

To construct an ileal conduit, a segment of terminal ileum (approximately 15cm) is isolated, preserving its blood supply. The remaining ileum is then reconstructed to restore bowel continuity. Both ureters, once divided from the bladder, are implanted into the proximal end of the segment of ileum, now known as the ileal conduit. The distal end of the conduit is brought out through the abdominal wall at a site marked by the stoma care nurse and surgeon before the operation. Implantation of the ureters may be done by one of several methods, but this largely depends on the technique preferred by the surgeon performing the operation. A fine silastic catheter or T-tube may be inserted through the conduit and placed across the uretero-ileal anastomosis to act as a splint and allow satisfactory drainage of the urine (see Figure 8.1). The

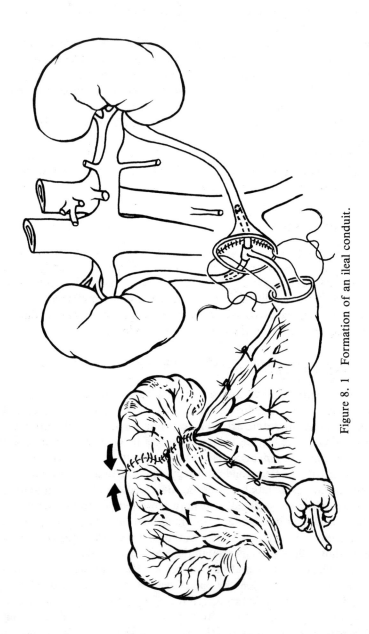

Figure 8. 1 Formation of an ileal conduit.

tubes slip out spontaneously or are removed by gentle traction 8–12 days following operation. The newly formed stoma is always swollen and oedematous at first, but this settles down after 10–14 days. It should be bright pink in colour, moist and shiny. A stoma which appears dark red or black indicates that the blood supply to the conduit is impaired. As the post-operative oedema resolves, the blood supply improves, but occasionally it is necessary to make a new conduit with a better blood supply.

Peristaltic action of the segment allows rapid emptying of the conduit, preventing significant reabsorption of urinary constituents, a major problem with ureterosigmoidostomy.

COLONIC CONDUIT

Transverse colon or sigmoid colon can be used as an alternative to ileum when constructing a urinary conduit. It has been found that there is less risk of stenosis and pyelonephritis when transverse colon is used, because of its rich blood supply, and it is usually preferred to sigmoid colon. Colonic conduits are often much larger than ileal conduits and are frequently sited on the left side of the abdomen.

CUTANEOUS URETEROSTOMY

In this procedure the ureters are brought to the surface of the skin as an alternative to an ileal or colonic conduit. Cutaneous ureterostomy is a simple, rapid procedure often preferred by surgeons for ill patients with poor renal function and dilated ureters. It may be permanent, temporary, single (Figure 8.2), bilateral (Figure 8.3), or double-barrelled (Figure 8.4). This method of urinary diversion avoids intestinal surgery and has no problems with electrolyte reabsorption and mucus production. However, ureterostomies are very prone to stomal stenosis and often require reconstruction. The creation of a good spout is difficult when using ureter, and there are often problems maintaining a leakproof seal around the stoma.

SITING OF THE STOMA

When preparing the patient for urinary diversion, it is important to select a good site for the stoma. Careful consideration must be given to

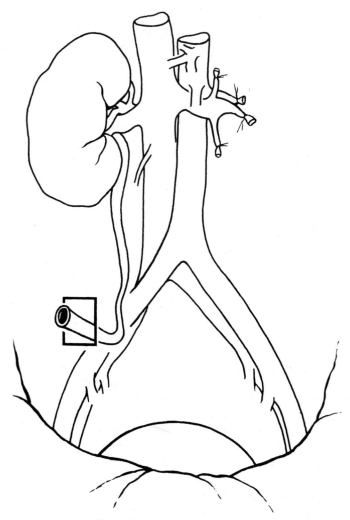

Figure 8.2   Single ureterostomy.

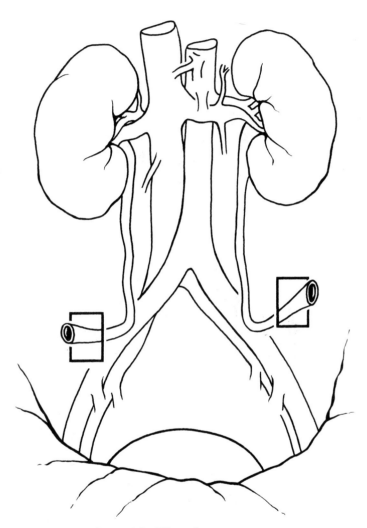

Figures 8.3   Bilateral ureterostomy.

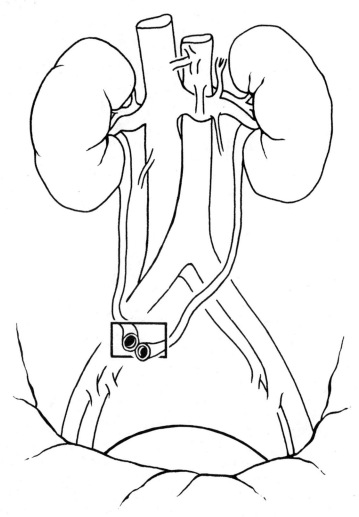

Figure 8.4 Double-barrelled ureterostomy.

the lifestyle of each patient: his work, pastimes and hobbies. Patients confined to wheelchairs, especially those with paraplegia or spina bifida, must be given extra consideration to ensure that the stoma is placed in a position which is comfortable and sufficiently flat to prevent leakage from the appliance. Further considerations in stoma siting have been dealt with in Chapter 4.

THE UROSTOMY APPLIANCE

The patient with a urinary diversion stoma will require an appliance which has special features that distinguish it from those used for colostomy or ileostomy. It must have an adhesive which prevents leakage and is not rapidly destroyed by urine. The appliance itself must be drainable, with an outlet which can be easily connected to night drainage, and must be of a size to allow 2–3 hours between emptying (see Figure 8.5).

The basic requirements for changing and disposing of appliances have been discussed in Chapter 4, and should be referred to before considering the additional needs of the urostomist.

The choice of urostomy appliance largely depends upon the individual requirements of each patient. There are various types available for use with urinary stomas: disposable, non-disposable, one-piece or two-piece. Some patients prefer an opaque bag, but in the immediate post-operative period the appliance of choice must be one which is transparent to allow observation of the new stoma, leakproof, non-irritant to the skin, comfortable to wear and easily connected to overnight drainage. A disposable one-piece appliance, of which there are many styles of varying capacity and gasket size, has become a popular choice for use in the immediate post-operative period.

The non-disposable two-piece appliance considered by many to be 'old-fashioned' is still used by some patients as a permanent appliance. It consists of a rubber flange attached to the abdomen by a double-sided adhesive plaster, and a rubber or plastic bag which is stretched over the flange. The rubber bags offer reliability for many patients, and are strong and hard wearing, and capable of holding large volumes of urine quite safely. A large capacity night bag may be applied in place of the smaller day bag.

Assembly of this system is time-consuming; the flanges are bulky and each component requires scrupulous maintenance to ensure absolute cleanliness.

Stoma Care

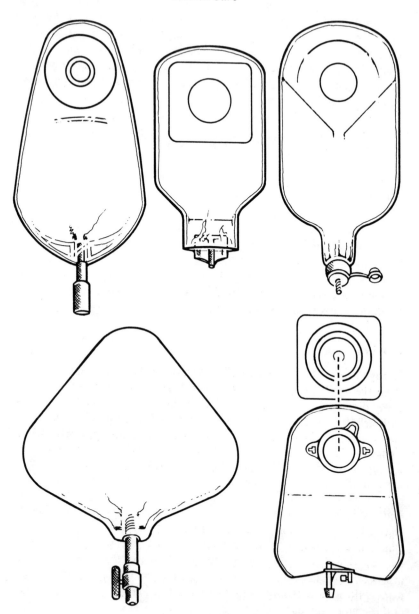

Figure 8.5   Urostomy appliances.

The modern disposable two-piece appliance offers similar advantages to those of the non-disposable variety and may incorporate an anti-reflux valve in the plastic bag. A two-piece appliance which combines a flange with a skin barrier material will offer additional protection to the skin and allow changing of the bag without removal of the flange. It allows access to the stoma when catheter specimens of urine are required, or for the removal of phosphate deposits. It is easily connected to bedside drainage, but the outlet tap is suitable only for patients with good eyesight and nimble fingers.

SKIN BARRIERS

Disposable appliances are designed to be applied directly to the skin by means of an adhesive faceplate. Occasionally, however, the application of a skin barrier is required to treat and prevent allergic reactions from these adhesives. Skin barriers may also be used to provide additional adhesion around the stoma by forming a watertight seal, and are available in many shapes and forms.

KARAYA

Karaya is probably the most well known of all skin barriers, and comes from the sap of a tree which grows in India. It is an integral part of many disposable appliances and may be used quite safely for patients with urinary stomas. It does dissolve, however, and the time it takes to do so varies from patient to patient. Some patients, especially those with very sensitive skins, may develop an allergic reaction to the karaya, in which case an alternative skin barrier must be used.

STOMAHESIVE

This is a very popular and successful type of skin protection, and is widely used to treat and prevent skin excoriation around the stoma. It has recently been incorporated in the design of a modern two-piece urostomy appliance and remains intact for several days, despite being constantly bathed in urine. It does, however, eventually dissolve and require changing. As a skin barrier, Stomahesive is particularly useful when managing flush ureterostomies and copious faecal fistulae.

When using Stomahesive it is important to ensure that the hole in the centre of the plaster is a snug fit for the stoma, without it being too tight and constricting the blood supply. Radial slits around the opening will prevent this, and enable the Stomahesive to mould into the contours of the skin. Too large an opening in any skin barrier will allow the urine from the stoma to bathe the peristomal skin, causing problems with irritation, excoriation and leakage.

RELIASEAL DISCS

These are very similar to Stomahesive, but are used mainly as a means of reinforcing the adhesive faceplate of one-piece appliances. They are stronger and usually longer-lasting than Stomahesive in the presence of urine. Other skin barriers include Hollister skin gel, Op-Site, Tincture Benzoin Co. and Skin Prep, and are available in tubes and sprays.

Many skin barriers remain intact for several days at a time, even though they are used as part of a urostomy appliance. A quick and easy method of applying a skin barrier is to attach it to the appliance faceplate first, and apply them both as a one-piece unit. Urine drips from the stoma at approximately 20–30 second intervals, and patients should be discouraged from restricting their fluid intake in order to control the output. It cannot be overemphasised that an increased intake helps to reduce the risk of urinary infection.

Various sealing agents are available to assist in the formation of a watertight seal around the gasket of the appliance; these include karaya powder, Orahesive powder and Orabase paste.

Some patients occasionally require more than a skin barrier to treat peristomal skin excoriation, especially when bacterial and fungal infections are present. Triamcinolone acetomide (Adcortyl spray) is particularly useful when used in conjunction with nystatin powder (Nystan) to reduce the inflammation and to treat the infection.

The Adcortyl spray should be applied to the inflamed skin (some smarting does occur), followed by the Nystan powder. Both are then sealed in with a skin barrier such as Op-Site spray, which also allows adhesion of the appliance. If necessary, this treatment may be repeated after 3–4 days.

Applying oily creams and ointment to the peristomal skin is inadvisable, as it will prevent the adhesion of most skin barriers, plasters and tapes.

NIGHT DRAINAGE SYSTEMS

It is common practice in hospital to attach a bedside drainage bag to the urostomy appliance for the continuous drainage of urine. The frequency of emptying the urostomy bag is greatly reduced, as is the risk of overflow and leakage. Most systems hold large volumes of urine, usually up to 2000ml, and are easily attached to an independent stand or hanger. There are various models available to choose from, some designed specifically for use with the same make of appliance (Surgicare Drainage System). Most systems have an integral outlet tap for quick and easy emptying, whereas others have to be emptied from the inlet tubing. Simpla S4 (Simpla Plastics), Meredith (Eschmann) and Surgicare's System 2 have a built-in non-return valve to prevent the backflow of urine.

One of the main advantages of bedside drainage is that it enables the patient to enjoy an undisturbed sleep without the worry of the appliance filling and needing to be emptied. The long connecting tube allows unrestricted movement in bed without it becoming entangled.

After discharge from hospital, some people choose to do without bedside drainage, preferring to empty the appliance once or twice during the night, especially if they have experienced 'accidents' when using the system previously.

Bedside drainage systems are usually designed to be re-used, and the length of time they last varies from system to system. Each morning the system should be washed out thoroughly, using hot soapy water, and rinsed well. Antiseptics and disinfectant are not essential, but a drop can be added to the bag itself if preferred. When the system becomes stained, or develops an odour, usually after 7–9 days, it should be disposed of in the same way as the urostomy pouches.

ODOUR

Odour is not such a major problem for urostomists as it is for patients with colostomies or ileostomies. Most modern appliances are made from odourproof material which prevents the passage of odour through the bag. However, urine which develops a strong odour is often infected, and the patient should be encouraged to increase his fluid intake.

Various deodorising agents are available for use with ostomy appliances, but are of little value to the patient with a urinary stoma.

Aerosol sprays such as Atmocol or Ozium are useful for freshening the air after each bag change.

Special consideration is given to everyday activities such as work, bathing, clothing, etc. These are covered in detail in Chapters 4 and 7.

URINARY INFECTION

Urinary infection is a major problem, whatever type of urinary diversion is selected. It may present as a general pyrexial illness with loin pain, rigors and vomiting, requiring treatment with the appropriate antibiotics; the urine is often cloudy, thick and offensive.

A sterile catheter specimen of urine taken from the conduit for culture will confirm or exclude the presence of organisms. The specimen must not be taken from the collecting bag, because this urine is nearly always contaminated, and culture will yield a positive result.

It is important to exclude mechanical problems within the conduit, particularly obstruction at skin level or at the uretero-ileal anastomosis. A large residual volume of urine present in the loop indicates an obstruction, and if too long a segment of ileum has been used for the conduit, a sump effect develops, allowing urine to stagnate and become infected.

Routine investigations such as intravenous pyelogram and loopogram are useful as a means of diagnosing mechanical problems such as these. A loopogram is a simple procedure which involves inserting a contrast medium into the conduit using a catheter; it shows up any obstruction at the uretero-ileal anastomosis or reflux up the ureter.

The normal pH of urine is 6.5 (slightly acid), but infected urine tends to become alkaline and predisposes to the formation of phosphate crystals on and around the stoma and appliance. If left unattended, these desposits can cause friction and bleeding from the stoma and subsequent ulceration and infection. Five per cent acetic acid (dilute household vinegar), either in the appliance or used to bathe the stoma, will help to acidify the urine and remove the deposits. Alternatively, Aci-Jel cream (1 per cent acetic acid base) may be applied to the stoma once or twice daily.

In the absence of mechanical problems, the patient should increase his fluid intake. The presence of organisms in a conduit specimen of urine does not necessarily require treatment with antibiotics. Many patients carry organisms without any danger to the urinary tract. Recurrent urinary infections can give rise to serious long term consequences such as pyelonephritis, calculus formation and eventual renal failure.

METHOD OF OBTAINING URINE SPECIMENS FROM AN ILEAL CONDUIT

When taking a catheter specimen of urine from an ileal conduit, care must be taken to ensure that bacteria from outside the stoma are not introduced into the conduit. This can be achieved by using an aseptic technique, and thoroughly cleansing the stoma with a mild antiseptic such as Betadine solution. A female polythene residual catheter which is semi-rigid (14FG or smaller) is inserted into the stoma, taking care not to be too forceful, as there is a small risk of perforating the ileum.

If the catheter does not pass into the conduit easily, gentle pressure applied around the stoma will help the spout to protrude and admit the catheter. Alternatively, the direction of the conduit can be found by inserting a finger into the stoma itself. The first few drops of urine should be discarded, and a sterile universal container used to catch the specimen.

SEX AND THE UROSTOMIST

Ileal conduit urinary diversion is no contra-indication of itself to normal sexual activity, normal full term pregnancy and raising a family. For example, a woman with a minor degree of spina bifida, who has had urinary diversion because of neurological impairment of her bladder, may still enjoy intercourse and have children without any undue risk. A patient who has just undergone urinary diversion may find the presence of the stoma embarrassing, but this may be overcome by simple explanation, the provision of a lightweight non-transparent urostomy appliance or cover, and a sympathetic, understanding partner. Problems with leakage from the urostomy bag can be avoided by emptying the bag completely before intercourse, wearing a new small-size 'activity' stoma pouch, and enjoying different positions for intercourse that avoid crushing the stoma or the appliance.

On the other hand, many patients with urinary diversion do have problems with intercourse, not because of the presence of the stoma, but because of the disease necessitating urinary diversion. Neurological disorders affecting the bladder may also affect the nerves required for sexual activity. Congenital abnormalities of the lower urinary tract are often associated with congenital anomalies of the internal and external genitalia. Operations such as cystectomy or anterior pelvic exenteration almost always render a man impotent and block ejaculation, and in women they reduce the size of the vagina and interfere with its sensation. Radical radiotherapy to pelvic organs may also cause impotence and reduce genital sensation in both sexes. It should also be remembered that many patients undergo urinary diversion at an age when sexual activity is decreasing. Some neurological diseases, the fear of recurrent cancer or recovery from major surgery or radiotherapy can also all cause a loss of libido.

Despite these various factors, some urostomy patients will retain a limited amount of sexual sensation which they wish to enjoy, or may have sexually active partners whom they would like to satisfy, despite their own impotence or inability to participate in 'normal' intercourse. A man may be impotent after cystectomy but still retain sufficient penile sensation to reach orgasm. A woman's vagina may be obliterated by radiation and surgery, and so be unsuitable for penile penetration, yet she may retain normal sensation in the clitoris. In this situation sexual stimulation with the fingers and some suitable lubricant, or oral intercourse, should be employed to obtain maximum pleasure for both partners. Similarly, for the urostomy patient who is totally incapacitated sexually but has a normal partner, such techniques, or the use of marital aids such as a vibrator, can provide a satisfactory alternative to the 'normal' mechanism. For the impotent urostomy patient with a sexually active wife, it is possible to insert a silastic splint inside the corpora cavernosa of the penis, thereby providing an erect organ and normal intercourse with penetration.

Many people, particularly older patients, do not indulge in these activities and require considerable psychological adjustment after their operation. Some are shocked or offended by suggestions of 'alternative' sexual techniques and prefer to accept the termination of their sexual activities. On the other hand, many patients with a new urostomy become frustrated or feel inadequate within their marriage and do not know where to seek advice. It is therefore important for doctors, stoma therapists and nurses to discuss with the patient the sexual aspects of urinary diversion, together with the other practical details of their operation and subsequent life with a stoma, both before and after surgery. Because of the particular problems involved, it may be advisable to see the patient and his or her partner together in the privacy of the ward office or the out-patient clinic, rather than talking about it with the patient on the conventional ward round.

Most patients with urinary diversion already have a family or are past the childbearing age, but it should be remembered that some urostomy patients may want to have a family, and adoption or Artificial Insemination by Donor may be considered.

The presence of urinary diversion by itself is no contra-indication to becoming an adoptive parent, but the underlying disease which necessitated diversion may mean that adoption of a family, or even a natural pregnancy, would be inadvisable.

QUESTIONS FOR DISCUSSION

1) Ileal conduit has become the most popular and successful method of urinary diversion. What are the advantages of this type of diversion compared to ureterosigmoidostomy?

2) What are the special features which distinguish the urostomy pouch from other ostomy appliances?

3) Phosphate deposits on and around the stoma may predispose to ulceration and bleeding. Explain why encrustation occurs, the best method of treatment and how it may be prevented.

4) Excoriation of the peristomal skin can be a problem regardless of the type of stoma. List the common causes of skin irritation and the most suitable methods of treatment.

5) What type of urostomy appliance is preferred in the immediate post-operative period following urinary diversion? Give the reasons why such an appliance is used.

6) Urinary tract infections are common among urostomists. What advice would you give a patient to help reduce the risk of urinary infection? What are the long term complications which may occur as a result of recurrent urinary infection?

7) Bleeding from the stoma easily occurs if it is damaged or harmed accidentally. What could be the cause of haematuria in a patient with an ileal conduit following cystectomy for a malignant bladder tumour?

Chapter 9

Paediatric Stoma Care

Children of all ages, from the newborn to the teenager, may require surgery which results in a stoma. Both temporary and permanent stomas of the types discussed in Chapters 3 and 8 are raised in children. The basic methods of care for bowel and urinary stomas outlined in Chapters 4 and 8 are also suitable for the child with a stoma, but psychological and social aspects of care must be tailored to meet the needs of each child and his family. Children in hospital should be nursed and doctored in an environment where staff are knowledgeable about their developmental needs as well as their stoma care. The effects of the primary condition, or the resulting periods in hospital, may have far-reaching consequences for the child whose mental and emotional development may be delayed, or even permanently damaged. Subsequent surgery will also disrupt family life, affecting not only the child and parents, but also the siblings.

Nursing and medical staff can do much to encourage the whole family to be involved with the child ostomist. Concentration by staff and parents on the needs of the child with a stoma, with exclusion or scant attention to the needs of other children in the family, is likely to result in difficulties in forming relationships for the other children later on. The parents' needs as individuals and as a couple are also important. Staff can help them accept they have a right to time for themselves, without feeling guilty about not spending every moment meeting the needs of the child with the stoma.

A full paediatric assessment is necessary to establish the extent of physical impairment in each child, and the difficulties which may arise over and above those which have already been outlined for adults.

CONDITIONS FOR WHICH STOMAS ARE RAISED IN CHILDREN

SPINA BIFIDA

This is a congenital defect in which vertebral arches fail to close, exposing the contents of the spinal canal posteriorly. The fissure usually occurs in the lumbosacral region. The contents of the canal may or may not protrude through the opening. Herniation of the intact meninges through the bony defect to form a sac containing cerebrospinal fluid and malformed nerve tissue is called a meningomyelocele. Where this sac ruptures, further nerve damage occurs. Motor and sensory loss at and below the level of the lesion is usually associated with this condition, and damage to nerves to the rectum and bladder is very common. (A meningocele with a thick walled sac with intact spinal cord rarely causes these problems.)

Hydrocephalus is almost always associated with the spinal lesion, and usually needs early surgical relief with a shunt (Spitz-Holter valve). However well this is treated, these children often have mildly clumsy hand function and a slightly reduced level of intelligence.

Incontinence of faeces from constipation with overflow is avoidable with regular management. Incontinence of urine, or retention of urine with overflow and severe back-pressure on the kidneys, may necessitate a urinary diversion, particularly in female children. The increasing use of the technique of intermittent self-catheterisation is likely to result in fewer urinary stomas for girls in the future. Boys can often be assisted in overcoming their urinary problems by fitting them with a penile appliance. Paediatric surgeons are becoming increasingly selective in their assessments of children for surgery. Lorber (1975) indicates that, despite the best of care, about half of the severely affected children will die, and the remainder stand a very high chance of being severely mentally retarded and confined to wheelchairs.

Where surgical diversion is necessary, there are two main by-pass operations which may be considered: ureterostomy, and formation of an ileal conduit. These have been discussed in Chapter 8.

IMPERFORATE ANUS

This is a congenital condition where there is no anal exit for faeces. Occasionally in girls and more commonly in boys there may be no alternative passage at all, and surgery will be required urgently to establish a right transverse colostomy, with subsequent laparotomy and pull-through procedure to provide an anal exit.

Imperforate anus may occur in combination with a recto-vaginal or recto-urethral fistula. Surgery is less urgent, as the faeces are expelled via the fistula. Treatment again usually consists of raising a right transverse colostomy prior to laparotomy and a pull-through operation. By the time the baby is six months old the colostomy can usually be closed and the baby is able to pass faeces via the rectum.

HIRSCHSPRUNG'S DISEASE OR AGANGLIONOSIS

The primary abnormality is a lack of ganglion cells in the wall of the gut. This abnormality extends proximally from the internal anal sphincter for a variable length of the bowel. In the majority of cases only the rectum plus sigmoid colon are aganglionic, but the lack of ganglion cells may be more extensive and on occasion extend into the small bowel. Associated congenital anomalies are frequent. The aganglionic section of bowel does not function normally, and fails to pass material along the lumen satisfactorily, resulting in incomplete obstruction and short episodes of complete obstruction of the bowel. The patient has a temporary ileostomy performed and the affected part of the colon is removed. The ileostomy is usually raised for about six months to ensure that the colon has healed, though the period of time can be as long as eighteen months. Newborn infants sometimes succeed in passing meconium and thereby relieve the obstruction for a time, but otherwise may present with complete intestinal obstruction at birth. The classical description of Hirschsprung's disease in infants is chronic constipation, abdominal distension and failure to thrive. The babies also often have a characteristic worried expression.

NECROTISING ENTEROCOLITIS

This condition may arise in small pre-term babies who have required major intensive care because of respiratory distress in the first few days of life. The cause of the bowel necrosis is not known. Treatment is conservative, where possible, as the bowel can recover if it is rested and if intravenous and antibiotic therapy is given. Surgery is required if perforation occurs, or if stricture of the bowel develops, and a colostomy or ileostomy may then be raised as a temporary stage in recovery.

ECTOPIA VESICAE

This is a congenital condition where the bladder is abnormally placed, opening on to, or protruding through, the abdominal wall. This is often associated with other congenital abnormalities, such as malposition or abnormal development of the sexual organs. Surgery is normally carried out to improve both the function and appearance of the areas involved. In some cases a urinary diversion is necessary.

ULCERATIVE COLITIS AND CROHN'S DISEASE

Children with these diseases occasionally require stoma surgery before adulthood.

SITING OF THE STOMA

This is as important for the child as for the adult, and the basic considerations common to both have been discussed in Chapter 4.

The child with spina bifida is likely to have several additional potential problem areas. These must be considered carefully when establishing possible stoma sites, if areas under strain or in contact with rigid wheelchairs, belts or calipers are to be avoided. The bony defect in the spine, combined with partially paralysed spinal muscles, very often results in a slowly developing abnormal spinal curve, either sideways to form a scoliosis or forwards to form a kyphosis. These children very easily become overweight, and the combined result is an abdomen with distorted rolls of fat. Even if this occurs before stoma surgery, it is not uncommon to find a once well-sited stoma at the bottom of a deep skin crease, as the child grows and his body shape alters. This can create many leakage problems, and surgery to resite the stoma is sometimes required.

Consideration must therefore be given to:
1) Any impairment of hand co-ordination which might make manipulation of appliance outlets difficult;
2) Any curvature of the spine, which may increase with age;
3) Calipers: their size and mode of fitment, both at the time of surgery and later as the child grows;
4) Any methods of assistance required by the child to get in and out of a wheelchair;
5) Actual or potential obesity caused by lack of exercise.

For such patients, a suitable method of establishing the best stoma site may be to apply bags before operation to several potentially suitable sites. These may be left in place for a period of time while the child returns to his normal daily activities. Later the bags will be examined, and sites rejected where the bag is found to be under strain or pulling away from the body.

CONSIDERATIONS IN STOMA CARE FOR CHILDREN

Care and support for the child ostomist and his family is of concern to all members of the health care team. The facilities which every child should have, which include play materials, access to school facilities or visiting teachers, visits from occupational therapists and physiotherapists and so on, are just as necessary for the child with a stoma as for other children.

Assessment of the child and his family will normally be made by nurses, doctors and other members of the team, particularly the medical social workers. The broad assessment required for every child will include physical, mental and emotional development, and patterns of behaviour in social activities as well as sleep, feeding and elimination patterns.

The assessment of the family and their needs is an integral part of good stoma care. The effect of the ostomist on the rest of the family, and of the family and environment on him, are important. It is also necessary to assess the degree of family stability under stress, and to establish ways of giving support which are seen by the family as useful and acceptable. Support will be necessary for parents as they face the implications of having a baby who looks different from the perfect infant that all parents expect to produce. Discrepancies between the parents' views of normal body image and elimination methods, and the reality for their baby, are often difficult for them to accept.

THE PARENTS' ROLE

In many children's wards the parents take an active part in their child's care, and continuation of this, once the parents feel they have mastered the basic methods of stoma care, will do much to boost their confidence.

It is advisable for the stoma care nurse, where available, to be involved in the case as soon as the likelihood of a stoma has been considered. In many cases the parents will use the stoma care nurse as their link between hospital and the community, knowing that they will receive help and support from her in the future.

Once the parents have accepted the necessity of the operation, they will need to be reassured that they will be taught how to look after the stoma. It will be here that the experienced nurse, by simplifying the procedure, will convince the parents that they will cope with the situation.

It must be shown that the materials required are simple and generally available in most homes, and that the procedure is not only simple but easily memorised and carried out. There is no set age at which a child can be taught to look after the stoma. This depends on the parents and their approval, as well as the individual child.

If the parents by their attitude show that the matter of looking after the stoma is simple, then more than likely the child will follow suit. The initial approach by the nursing and medical staff is so important to all concerned. Acknowledgement of the mental stress that will be caused in the initial stages to the parents and also, according to the child's age, to the child, can do much to reduce their anxiety. The aim must be at all times to increase the confidence of the parents and the child to cope with the situation, so that the child will be able to live as near a normal life as possible.

BAGS VERSUS NAPPIES

Where a very young baby has to have a stoma, the reaction of the parents will normally be that nappies are the easiest solution, since nappies are normally associated with babies at this age. It should be remembered that nappies can cause further complications to the existing stoma problems. There is a danger of skin deterioration and eventually deep excoriation, due to urine and faeces being in constant contact with the skin. If bags are used from the onset, even on very young children, the likelihood of skin problems can be minimised. By using the bag from the onset the child adapts to wearing it at an early stage, and as time goes on this will increase the confidence of both the child and parents. Normally there will be little skin excoriation if the correct procedures are carried out in looking after the stoma.

In the child who is of an age when nappies would normally not be worn, confidence will be built up by using bags, so that the family can go ahead with holidays and daily activities as an ordinary family unit. Fear of offending other people with odour from the stoma effluent may

be removed by using odour resistant bags. Parents who have a child
with a stoma are often inhibited from allowing him to engage in normal
social activities, for fear of what other people may think.

SPECIAL SCHOOLING

The presence of a stoma does not automatically mean that a child
requires special schooling or facilities. Where there is no physical or
mental impairment, attendance at a normal school may be encouraged,
but help must be available if the stoma needs attention during school
hours. The majority of spina bifida children attend a special school for
the physically handicapped, where they have the opportunity to gain
confidence and independence. There are specialised trained medical
and educational staff who, in liaison, ensure that each child is allowed
and encouraged to attain a degree of confidence and independence that
is within the individual's capability. Back-up services in the schools
normally include occupational therapy, physiotherapy and speech
therapy departments. The educational requirements are not forgotten;
the school's equipment is designed to take into account the disabilities
of the children. The ratio of teachers and helpers to children is far
higher than in the non-specialised school, usually about 1:10, thus
providing the opportunity for individual attention when it is most
needed.

It is with this background that an increase in the child's confidence
and independence can be built. Outings will be arranged so that the
children go out and meet other people of all ages, without their parents
always being present. It will also be in this environment that they will
take part in physical activities which will show them that they need not
be deprived of taking part in many activities which other children
enjoy. They will of course learn that some activities will have to be
modified to take into account their physical disabilities. The aim of all
concerned must be to train each child towards living as full and normal
a life as he can attain.

The school nurse will encourage the child to learn how to change his
own appliance. She will support the parents as they encourage the child
to change his appliance at home as well, instilling the procedure into
him and giving him the necessary increase in confidence and independence.

SUPPORT FOR THE PARENTS AND CHILD

The prime support in the early stages will be the ward nursing staff who hand over to the community nursing team on discharge. Many health visitors have particular knowledge of handicapped children and their needs, and are a source of information and support for both child and family. Both teams work in close liaison with the local stoma care nurse if one is in post, and also with the family practitioner. The social worker will give relevant information about the social services normally available, and often provides on-going support to the family.

Specialised associations have been formed by parents and interested parties with the particular disabilities in mind. Here parents can meet others in the same position as themselves, who share many of their feelings and problems.

Association for Spina Bifida and Hydrocephalus (ASBAH)
This is an association for patients with these conditions, and their families (see page 205). Advice is offered about appliances, aids, and the availability of allowances or grants.

Support is given to both patient and family to build up each individual's confidence and expertise, in as wide a range of normal activities as possible. The special holidays which ASBAH run help many individuals on their way to independence.

Youth organisations
There are various youth organisations that make provision for the handicapped to take part in their activities. They often modify activities so that the handicapped may take part in most of the functions that are carried out. Use of these organisations may enable further steps forward to be taken towards confidence and independence.

All spina bifida children seem to enjoy swimming, even though they suffer the handicap of being paralysed below the site of the spinal defect. The natural buoyancy of the water gives them confidence, and can often put them on a par with children without this handicap. A Challenge Club exists in most areas – its function is to help the physically handicapped to participate in various sports competing against other children with similar disabilities. These are normally activities that can be carried out whilst sitting in a wheelchair, and include such sports as archery, discus-throwing and wheelchair racing. Other sports that are increasing in popularity are wheelchair dancing and also horse riding.

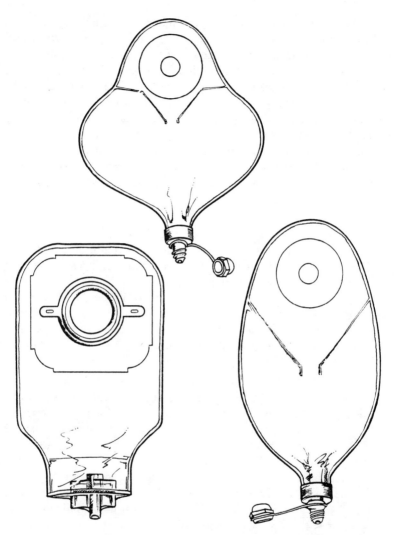

Figure 9.1 Small urostomy appliances suitable for children.

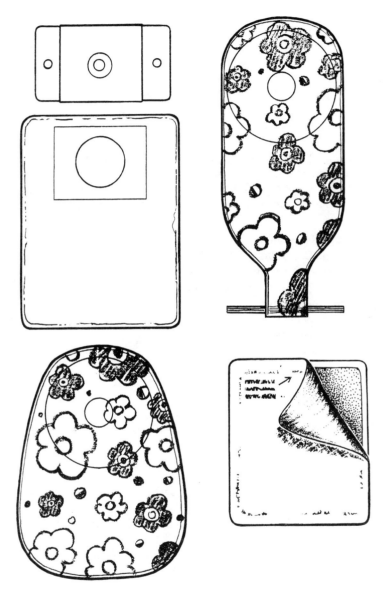

Figure 9.2 Small drainable and closed appliances with skin protective aids: suitable for children with bowel stomas.

APPLIANCES

There are very few appliances designed especially with the young patient in mind, particularly regarding the size of the appliance (Figures 9.1 and 9.2). One also has to consider that the hand co-ordination of a patient with spina bifida, who has had a Spitz-Holter valve inserted, can be impaired and difficulty in managing small taps may arise. Such patients will require a belt to support their urinary appliance. Extra care must be exercised in placing the belt so that it does not apply pressure to any protrusions of the spinal column.

An appliance should always be used in conjunction with adequate skin protection. Where Stomahesive or a Comfort Plate is used, the appliance can be applied to the skin aid, and both applied as one piece.

The needs of the child with a stoma must always be seen within the network of the family. Perception of the growing child as an increasingly independent individual is difficult for most parents, and may be more difficult for those whose child has a stoma. Support for each child and his family, as they learn to accept that a stoma rarely curtails independence, is an integral part of the role of the nurse working in paediatric stoma care.

REFERENCE

Lorber J. 1975. Ethical problems in the management of myelomeningocele and hydrocephalus. *Journal of the Royal College of Physicians of London 10*, No. 1, 17.

QUESTIONS FOR DISCUSSION

1) For what reason are stomas formed in children and not in adults? Name two conditions.
2) What do you consider is the most important point to aim for when dealing with the older child on the subject of the application of appliances?
3) Can you name voluntary supportive groups available to parents and child alike?
4) What advantages does a spina bifida patient gain by attending a special physically handicapped school?

5) What possible method could be used to establish the most suitable site for a stoma in the case of a spina bifida patient?

6) If nappies are used on the very young baby, what is the main problem to look for?

7) If there is a likelihood of a child requiring a stoma, when do you consider the stoma care nurse should be involved?

8) What type of sport do most spina bifida patients enjoy?

9) What is the classical description associated with Hirschsprung's disease?

10) Is a stoma always permanent?

Chapter 10

The Care of Fistulae and Drain Sites

A fistula may be defined as an abnormal congenital or acquired communication between two hollow organs, or between a hollow organ and skin.

Fistulae that occur between gut and skin (enterocutaneous) are considered in this chapter. In many aspects an enterocutaneous fistula is similar to a stoma, and presents many of the problems of an ileostomy flush with the skin. Unlike a stoma, a fistula is usually a complication of disease or surgery rather than part of a planned surgical procedure.

CAUSES AND CLASSIFICATION OF FISTULAE

The two most common causes of fistulae are anastomotic leakage following surgery or inadvertent injury to the gut at surgery. The anastomosis leaks either because the sutures become disrupted, or because an abscess develops at the site of anastomosis. The most common form of anastomosis to break down is that following anterior resection, and many surgeons will protect the anastomosis with a defunctioning colostomy.

Following a polya type gastrectomy (Billroth II) the duodenal stump may become disrupted and give rise to a duodenal fistula. A duodenal fistula may also result from injury to the duodenum during a right hemicolectomy or right nephrectomy.

Gastric fistulae are not as common, but can follow gastrectomy where leakage occurs at the gastric suture line.

Fistulae are a common complication of Crohn's disease, and usually arise from the small bowel following surgery. Less common are faecal fistulae in diverticular disease, where an abscess develops in the colon and discharges onto the skin, into the vagina (recto-vaginal) or into the bladder (vesico-colic).

Irradiation damage to the small or large bowel may occur during radiotherapy to the pelvic region and give rise to fistulae. Usually they are internal, often between the rectum and vagina (recto-vaginal), or between the rectum and the bladder (recto-vesical).

Trauma to the pancreas may give rise to pancreatic fistulae, but provided there is no proximal obstruction to the pancreatic duct most of these will close spontaneously. Although fluid loss is not usually a problem, rapid digestion of the skin occurs because of the enzymes secreted.

A biliary fistula may occur following surgery to the biliary tree, or trauma to the liver and bile ducts. T-tube drainage following exploration of the common bile duct is an example of a controlled temporary fistula.

Urinary fistulae may occur after surgery on the renal pelvis and ureter, or following bladder surgery and in particular trans-vesical prostatectomy.

MUCOUS FISTULA

Sometimes following a total colectomy and ileostomy the rectum is not removed but left in situ, and the proximal end of the rectum is brought out on to the abdominal wall. This is known as a mucous fistula. It may be necessary for the patient to wear a drainable appliance to collect the mucous discharge. If the discharge is minimal, a small gauze dressing or a stoma cap can be worn. At a later stage the rectum may be removed, or the ileum can be rejoined to the rectal stump to form an ileo-rectal anastomosis.

PROBLEMS

The discharge of enteric contents, usually through a recent laparotomy incision or drainage site, presents a serious nursing problem. The magnitude of the problem will depend on the amount and the site of origin of the discharge.

Duodenal, jejunal and ileal fistulae present the greatest problem, with a high output which will rapidly digest the surrounding skin. The higher the small bowel fistula is situated, the greater will be the loss of enzyme-rich fluid, causing severe excoriation of the skin. If the opening on the abdominal wall is an isolated drain site, protection of the skin is not too difficult. If the abdomen is severely scarred, with partial or total dehiscence of a laparotomy incision, management is more difficult.

MANAGEMENT OF FISTULAE EFFLUENT

For the patient, the constant discharge of fluid, which saturates the skin and rapidly leads to painful excoriation, is the most distressing symptom of his illness. The nursing staff must make every attempt to protect the skin by preventing the effluent from coming into contact with it.

In the past the skin was protected with aluminium paste or a variety of barrier creams, and bulky dressings were used in an attempt to contain the discharge. Some surgeons used sump suction drainage to divert the discharge, although others felt this increased the amount of drainage. In the main, dressings with or without suction were far from effective in the management of the fistulae. Within a few days of the fistula arising, the patient's skin was digested by the effluent, and not only the immediate area surrounding the fistula but often the whole abdomen became raw and inflamed. If leakage was excessive the soreness often extended into the groins, genital area and buttocks. Dressings required frequent changes, as did the patient's night-clothes and bed-clothes. Patients quickly became depressed and the nurses frustrated.

In recent years, with improved stoma care together with the availability of a wide range of stomal appliances, a drainable type of appliance has proved to be effective in the management of fistulae. For a small fistula, any drainable type appliance can be used, but for a large one and especially those occuring along laparotomy incisions, the styles illustrated in Figure 10.1 are of value.

The use of appliances has several advantages over dressings. The surrounding skin can be completely protected with a skin protective, e.g. Stomahesive, so that the effluent does not contaminate the skin. When dressings are used they allow the discharge to remain in contact with the skin. As already discussed, unless drainage is minimal even the bulkiest dressings never adequately contain the discharge, and some always manages to escape the dressings and ooze over the abdomen. If the effluent is faecal there is the added problem of odour, which is embarrassing for the patient, other patients and staff. With an odour-proof appliance this problem is easily controlled. The medical staff and biochemist not only need to know the volume of output, but often want

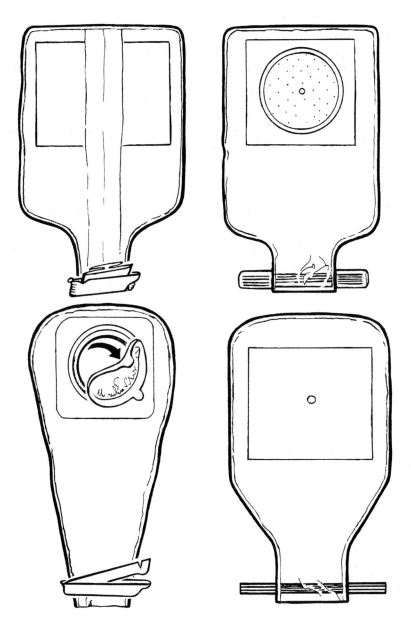

Figure 10.1 Four examples of drainable appliances which are frequently used in the management of fistulae.

to analyse the nitrogen and electrolyte content. With dressings such analysis is impossible, for although the dressing can be weighed before and after use and the volume of output estimated, the leakage which escapes the dressing cannot be assessed.

SKIN CARE AND APPLIANCES

The aim of skin care is to prevent the fistula discharge from acting on the skin by applying a protective agent. Stomahesive squares, karaya blankets and karaya paste are most commonly used, either on their own or in combination.

There is no one way of dressing a fistula, and each one has to be assessed on an individual basis. The site of origin and nature of output will determine what protective agent is used. A high output duodenal fistula, rich in enzymes, will require more skin protection than a low output colonic fistula. Similarly the high output fistula will require a larger appliance than the low output fistula. If the fistula exit point lies in proximity to a bony prominence, an appliance with a hard flange is unsuitable because it will not lie flat over the bone. A plain adhesive type bag is then used. If the fistula lies close to another dressing or drain site one should aim not to overlap the two, and then choose an appliance with a small area of adhesive. If the fistula has two exit points it is necessary to decide whether it is feasible to contain both in one appliance, if the medical staff are in agreement, or whether it is possible to use two appliances without overlap. It is important to ask the patient if he is allergic to any adhesives or skin protective agents before using them.

PROCEDURE

This is identical whether appliances or protective agents are used alone or in combination. One must ensure that the surrounding skin is cleansed and thoroughly dried. This can prove difficult if the fistula is continually discharging, and an assistant will be necessary. If the exit point is small, one or several cotton wool buds can be placed in the cavity, and this will momentarily stop the fistula discharging. For a larger fistula gauze swabs can be inserted into the cavity, but if the output is high even this will be inadequate. Under these circumstances, an assistant using a large syringe or a suction catheter can temporarily divert the effluent. This is not always easy – the assistant must be vigilant, and ready to cope with a sudden spurt of effluent. If the patient has just had a drink the problem is aggravated. Avoidance of oral fluids immediately prior to dressings is therefore advisable.

Once the skin is dried, the shape of the orifice should be cut out of the sheet of Stomahesive or karaya. This is not difficult if the orifice is small and isolated. But if there are several, or if the fistula extends the

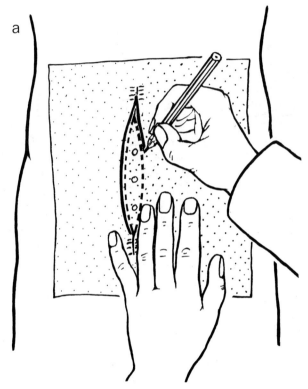

Figure 10.2 Application of Stomahesive and a drainable appliance on a burst abdominal wound with multiple fistulae. a) The shape of the orifice is traced on a template.

length of a laparotomy incision, one needs to trace the shape on to a template (Figure 10.2a). This can be done easily, and the polythene bag containing the Stomahesive or karaya is well used here. It is possibly best to do this before finally drying the skin, because it is difficult to trace around the edges if there is a suction catheter in situ. The template can be saved and re-used, but one must always check that there has been no change in the fistula shape before re-using it.

Before applying the skin protective agent, and to ensure that this does not lift at the skin edges, one can pipe a border of karaya paste around the edges of the orifice (Figure 10.2b). Any gulleys or crevices

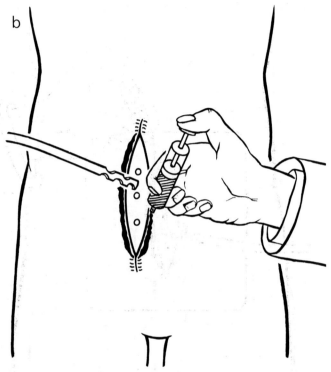

Figure 10.2   b) Karaya paste is piped around the edge of the orifice. A suction catheter is used to divert effluent so it does not spill onto the karaya.

should be filled before applying the skin protective agent. There are a number of different ways of doing this, such as using a protective paste, small pieces of karaya or small pieces of Stomahesive. If using karaya paste, the paste is first put into a syringe and then piped into the gulleys as one would use a cake-icing set. If the surrounding skin is already excoriated and inflamed, the patient will complain that the karaya paste burns. He must be reassured that this is short-lived and that it is worth the few seconds discomfort if the appliance adheres, thus keeping him dry and comfortable. If the excoriation is very severe and a large amount of paste is required, it may be necessary for the patient to have analgesia. Entonox is ideal, if available, as it is both extremely effective and can be rapidly controlled by the patient to meet his individual requirements. This method has obvious advantages over other routes of analgesic administration. The karaya paste should be allowed to dry for

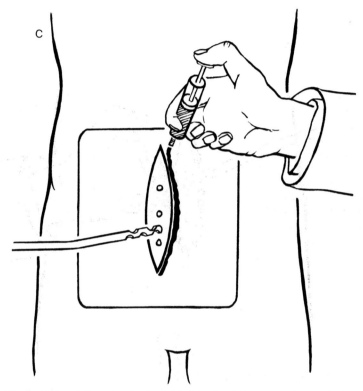

Figure 10.2   c) Stomahesive is applied to the abdomen, and more karaya paste is piped onto the Stomahesive at the orifice opening. Suction is also used at this stage to prevent leakage.

several minutes before the Stomahesive/karaya sheet is applied. Once it is in situ some pressure must be applied to ensure that the sheet adheres, particularly around the edges of the orifice. When one applies pressure to the abdomen, the fistula may pour, so one must be ready to cope with the sudden gush of fluid. The patient should be asked to avoid coughing during this period, because this will also activate the fistula.

If there are still any obvious gulleys when the Stomahesive is in situ, more karaya paste should be applied using a syringe (Figure 10.2c).

The appliance of choice is then quickly applied (Figure 10.2d). If the appliance adhesive has a protective backing paper it is simpler to peel this off gradually, sticking the adhesive down as one goes along, rather than taking all the paper off before applying the bag.

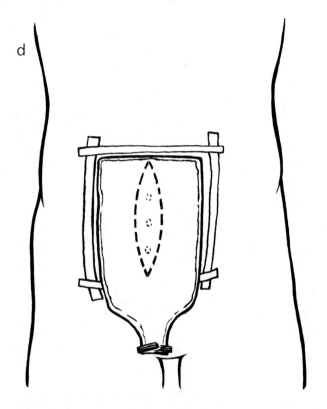

Figure 10.2 d) A bag is applied. The edge of the Stomahesive is made more secure by the application of hypo-allergenic tape.

Once the bag is in situ with a satisfactory seal there are certain points to note. The bag must be checked and emptied frequently, because if it is allowed to become too full the weight of the fluid will drag it off the skin. If the patient is sufficiently well, it is worthwhile teaching him to empty the appliance as he will usually empty it more frequently than the nursing staff. Unfortunately, some nurses are under the impression that the bag has to be completely full before it is emptied. The bag should be drained before turning or moving the patient as a sudden change of position may force the fluid from one side of the bag to the other, causing leakage. The night staff should be asked to empty the bag frequently throughout the night. Many dislike disturbing the sleeping patient and this results in the bag becoming overfull, with consequent leakage necessitating a total change of bag and bedclothes. At present none of the available appliances have a continuous drainage system. It may be possible to use a urinary appliance for a fistula, and then the continuous drainage system can also be used. Unfortunately the narrow outlet of a urinary appliance sometimes becomes blocked, and it may be worth devising one's own system. Mahoney (1976) describes a method of attaching a wide bore tube to the appliance using a loop of elastic and adhesive tape, and this is ideal. The proximal end of the tube can then be attached to a catheter drainage bag. If this method is used the nursing staff must check the drainage system frequently, because the tube may become blocked or kinked and the system then fails.

If the Hollister appliance with the inspection cap is used, one can remove the cap daily to inspect the Stomahesive or karaya for disintegration around the orifice. If there is evidence of disintegration, karaya paste can be re-applied. If there is extensive disintegration, the whole appliance needs changing. If an appliance stays in situ and is leakproof for several days it is tempting to leave it another day, if only so that one can say, 'I kept it on *x* number of days'. With experience one learns that it is better to change the appliance before it leaks, rather than when it leaks. It is amazing how quickly a patient is demoralised again if his appliance does leak. Experienced patients usually have some indication that it is going to leak, because they will experience a burning sensation under the protective agent as the fistula fluid seeps under the Stomahesive or karaya.

DRESSINGS

Occasionally, despite all one's ingenuity, a suitable appliance to cope with a fistula cannot be found, and one then has to revert to the use of dressings. The skin must still be protected – if Stomahesive will adhere it should be used, and failing this a good barrier cream. Dressings can then be applied but must be changed frequently. Charcoal impregnated dressings may eliminate the problem of odour but are not totally effective. The subtle use of air fresheners and air wicks may help, but nothing is as effective as odour-proof appliances.

CARE OF DRAIN SITES

Any drain site draining fluid which may cause skin excoriation can be managed in the same way as a fistula. A small piece of Stomahesive can be applied around the drain site and a drainable bag applied. Even when drainage is as minimal as 5ml in 24 hours some patients would prefer an appliance to dressings, especially if the drainage is malodorous.

It may be necessary for some patients to be discharged from hospital with a low output fistula, and the patient can then be taught how to apply the bag and empty it.

GENERAL MANAGEMENT AND NUTRITION

The successful management of a high output intestinal fistula demands a specific management plan. Chapman (1964) states his priorities in treatment of intestinal fistulae.

First Priority (0–12 hours)
1) Correct blood volume deficiency;
2) Drain obvious and easily accessible abscesses;
3) Control fistula, protect skin
   a) sump,
   b) bag.

Second Priority (0–48 hours)
1) Correct electrolyte imbalance;
2) Replace daily fluid and electrolyte losses;
3) Begin intravenous nutritional programme.

Third Priority (1–6 days)
1) Passage of feeding tube beyond fistula;
2) Feeding jejunostomy;
3) Continual search for and drainage of obvious abscesses if these appear.

Fourth Priority (after 5–14 days +)
Major surgical intervention:
1) To find occult sepsis;
2) To close or bypass the fistula.

When a fistula first appears, the plan of action should be initiated immediately. If treatment is delayed one has a septic, anaemic, nutritionally depleted and often dehydrated patient.

In the past, gastro-intestinal fistulae were associated with a considerable mortality and morbidity rate. Edmunds (1960) found a mortality rate of 62 per cent for gastric and duodenal fistulae, 54 per cent for small bowel fistulae and 16 per cent for colonic fistulae. The most common causes of death were malnutrition and electrolyte imbalance.

It is now recognised that adequate nutrition is the key to reduced mortality of patients with fistulae. As soon as a fistula is discovered nutritional support should be started.

INTRAVENOUS FEEDING

The ability to supply large amounts of calories and nitrogen through a central venous catheter has revolutionised the management of patients with fistulae. The average patient can receive 2000–3000 calories in the form of glucose and fat emulsion, and 10–12g of nitrogen, mainly as synthetic L-form amino acids daily. Table 10.1 lists some intravenous feeding preparations.

Table 10.1   Intravenous feeding preparations.

		Volume	Kilocalories
Glucose	50%	500ml	1000
Fructose	20%	500ml	400
Intralipid	20%	500ml	1000

		Volume	Nitrogen (g)
Aminosol	10%	500ml	6.5
Aminosol/fructose/ ethanol		500ml	2.12
Vamin with fructose		500ml	4.7

Infection is a frequent complication of intravenous feeding and catheter care is of the utmost importance. A strict regime of catheter care should be agreed upon by the medical and nursing staff. An occlusive dressing at the catheter site should be changed daily together with the intravenous giving set. Mechanical difficulties and complications from catheter placement are inevitable, even in the most experienced hands. These include pneumothorax, inadvertent placement of the catheter within the thoracic space, and catheter fracture and blockage. Too rapid intravenous feeding may result in hyperglycaemia, and urine should be tested 4-hourly for glucose estimation together with regular blood sugars.

ELEMENTAL DIETS

Because of the complications of intravenous feeding, nutrition should be maintained via the gastrointestinal tract as early as possible. After an initial course of intravenous feeding, an elemental diet is gradually introduced.

An elemental diet is a pre-digested diet which is almost completely absorbed in the upper gastrointestinal tract and which does not stimulate biliary, pancreatic or intestinal secretion. Examples of commercial elemental diets available in the United Kingdom are Flexical, Vivonex and Vivonex H.N. Table 10.2 shows the basic composition of Vivonex per 100 calories.

Table 10.2   Basic composition of Vivonex per 100 calories.

Constituent	Content
Carbohydrate	212g (glucose)
Protein	20g
Fat	0.87g
Sodium	55mmol
Potassium	30mmol
Chloride	76mmol
Magnesium	8mmol
Calcium	11.1mmol

Because of the high concentration of osmotically active particles (hypertonicity), too rapid introduction of an elemental diet may cause complications. The hypertonic solution draws water into the gut, causing diarrhoea and electrolyte imbalance. Elemental diets should therefore be administered slowly and diluted, gradually increasing the concentration so that the body can adapt to the hypertonic material.

The diet may be taken orally, via a naso-gastric tube or through a feeding gastrostomy or jejunostomy. In the case of a distal ileal fistula or colonic fistula the diet can be taken by mouth. For a more proximal fistula, such as gastric or duodenal, a feeding jejunostomy should be raised distal to the fistula.

If the diet is to be taken orally, palatability is a real problem and the patient will require a great deal of encouragement to take it. With the assistance of the dietitian, jellies and ice lollies can be prepared from the elemental diet and flavourings will improve the taste and appearance. The patient should be advised to sip the diet slowly using a straw. The diet should be kept ice-cold as this also improves palatability. If the patient cannot take the diet orally, a fine naso-gastric tube should be passed and the diet should be slowly infused to avoid overloading the gastrointestinal tract.

Providing digestion is normal, a far cheaper diet can be given consisting of protein hydrolysates with glucose polymers and medium chain triglycerides (Allison, 1975). These diets can be prepared daily by the hospital dietitian, and apart from the cost advantage they can be made up on an individual basis to meet the patient's requirements. Table 10.3 is an example of an Allison's Type Regime.

Table 10.3   Example of an Allison's Type Regime.

82g	Casilan (whole protein)
400g	Caloreen (glucose polymer)
30ml	M.C.T. (medium chain triglycerides)
1	Egg yolk (to provide essential fatty acids)
8g	Mineral mixture (including magnesium, iron, copper, zinc)
Plus	Vitamins
	Sodium
	Potassium

Again, like the elemental diet, this type of diet should be gradually introduced to the patient otherwise he may complain of nausea and diarrhoea.

MEDICATION

Most patients with fistulae have a prolonged hospital stay, with the attendant risk of various infections. Antibiotics should only be used when absolutely necessary. Although medication is not routinely given to control fistula output, it may be necessary for the patient to have medication, e.g. codeine phosphate, to help control diarrhoea caused by a liquid diet. Codeine phosphate syrup may be added and is effective in helping to control output. Similarly if the patient requires, or has had, excessive resection of the small bowel, then large doses of codeine phosphate or loperamide will be necessary to control the diarrhoea.

If the terminal ileum is resected vitamin B_{12} replacement is necessary, and although the patient will usually have 18 months' reserve stores it is usual to start therapy immediately.

PSYCHOLOGICAL CARE

Fistulae do not heal overnight. In MacFayden's (1973) study of sixty-one patients treated with parenteral hyperalimentation, 72.1 per cent closed in 38.5 days.

Any patient discharging gastric or faecal fluid from an abdominal orifice will at least begin to lose heart, and may often become depressed. Since most fistulae are a complication of surgery or disease the patient sees it as a setback impeding his progress.

If the abdominal orifice is large, and in particular if there is complete wound dehiscence, patients cannot believe that it will eventually heal, and they need a lot of reassurance from the medical and nursing staff. Sometimes a visit from a past patient who has completely recovered and survived the regime may help.

It is very important for the nursing staff to use every trick of the trade to ensure that the patient can be fitted with a leak-proof, odour-proof appliance. This in itself will do much for morale, for there is nothing more demoralising for the patient than to be continually reminded of the fistula by inadequate dressings that are continually leaking. Patients sometimes over-react when an appliance leaks, and can be extremely critical of the nurse who fitted the appliance. Every effort must be made by the nursing staff to understand the patient's attitude, which at times may appear unreasonable.

Sometimes when a fistula is beginning to close there may be minimal drainage in a 24 hour period, and the patient will obviously be delighted. However, the following day drainage may increase and the patient will be discouraged unless he is reassured that this variation is normal and may continue for several days.

Long periods of intravenous hyperalimentation, whether or not combined with elemental diets, are unpleasant and this will add to the patient's low morale. He will crave for solid food and once again every effort must be made to understand the patient's feelings and needs. Ideally these patients should not be placed in the ward where food is served, or next to patients who are eating normal food. Nursing fistulae patients can be extremely demanding, physically and mentally. There is nothing more demoralising for a nurse than to have spent an hour fitting an appliance only to hear the patient say as she walks off the ward, 'Nurse, it's leaking'. On the other hand, it is very rewarding to fit an appliance and to go along the following day to see the patient beaming and to hear him say, 'First dry night in weeks'.

REFERENCES

Allison, S. P. 1975. Elemental Diets. *The Lancet 2*, 507–8.

Chapman, Richard, Foran, Robert and Dunphy, Englebert J. 1964. Management of intestinal fistulas. *American Journal of Surgery 108*, 157–62.

Edmunds, L. H., Jr, Williams, G. M. and Welch, C. E. 1960. External fistulae arising from the gastrointestinal tract. *Ann. Surg. 152*, 445–73.

MacFayden, Bruce V., Jr, Dudrick, Stanley J. and Ruberg, Robert L. 1973. Management of gastrointestinal fistulas with parenteral hyperalimentation. *Surgery 74*, No. 1, 100–5.

Mahoney, J. M. 1976. *Guide to Ostomy Nursing Care*, 151–2. Little, Brown.

QUESTIONS FOR DISCUSSION

A 56-year-old lady is admitted to your ward with a *high output* fistula.

1) List four possible causes of a high output fistula.
2) What special nursing care would this lady require?
3) What advantages are there from using a drainable appliance to collect fistula fluid rather than dressings?
4) a) List three methods by which this patient may be fed.
   b) List the advantages and disadvantages of each method.

Chapter 11

Irrigation

Stoma care has changed dramatically over the past few years, with medical and nursing staff taking a much greater interest in improving the quality of life for the colostomy patient. Colostomy appliances have also evolved from bulky rubber bags to the new lightweight, odour-proof, non-allergic, disposable pouches. Even with such progress, an irregular faecal evacuation, and having to wear a permanent appliance on the abdomen, are worrying and frightening prospects for most colostomists.

Some control of the colostomy action, odour and faeces can be achieved by dietary restrictions, avoiding such foods as onions, 'greens', peas and beans, eggs and fish, by excluding beer, and by adding methyl cellulose and bran to the diet. Devlin *et al.* (1971) reported that 50 per cent of colostomists practised dietary restrictions to promote colostomy control.

The irrigation or wash-out method to produce a continent colostomy has not been widely used in Britain, although in the United States approximately 90 per cent of colostomists favour this method. In the past doctors have been reluctant to recommend the procedure, because of the possibility of bowel perforation when introducing the hard rubber catheter into the colon.

With the advent of purpose-built irrigation kits with a reservoir, clear tubing and a soft plastic introductory cone, this complication has been minimised. Soft tubes are available for irrigation, but the cone method is recommended.

The principle of irrigation of the colostomy is to introduce water into the distal half of the colon via the stoma, with a soft plastic cone to provide a safe leakproof junction. The water distends the colon, causing contraction, which in turn evacuates the faecal matter, which then passes through the long drain into the toilet pan.

The patient gets complete colostomy control with this method, and has no faecal evacuations between irrigations. Irrigation is necessary every twenty-four hours, and for some patients eventually every forty-eight hours.

There will be no necessity to wear an appliance when the technique has been mastered. The stoma is covered with lubricated gauze or a stoma cap, to protect the stoma and to collect the mucus secretion. Therefore, this method of colostomy control is economical of equipment.

A normal diet can be taken with no restrictions of any foods; flatus and odour are minimised. With the problems of colostomy control overcome, patients are much happier and become more confident and active.

SUITABILITY FOR IRRIGATION

The irrigation method is not suitable for all colostomists, and should never be used for ileostomists. Careful selection of patients by the surgeon and stoma care nurse is essential.

Patients with a sigmoid colostomy following abdomino-perineal excision of the rectum are the most suitable candidates for the irrigation technique. This is because the aim of no stomal action between irrigations is best achieved when evacuation of more solid faeces takes place from a sigmoid colostomy. Where the distal half of the colon is not functioning, as with an ascending or transverse colostomy, elimination of sufficient bowel contents to provide an action-free twenty-four hour period is rarely possible.

Patients who are *not* suitable for learning to irrigate include:

1) Those with ascending or transverse colostomies;
2) Those with Crohn's disease, where regular stimulation of contraction of the bowel might cause a flare-up of the disease;
3) Patients with diverticulitis, where perforation of the bowel can occur;
4) Patients with irritable bowel syndrome, where irrigation may result in abdominal pain and spasm;
5) Very elderly patients;
6) Those with poor sight or arthritic hands;
7) Mentally defective patients;
8) Those with residual or recurrent cancer.

Above all, the patient himself must wish to use the irrigation technique. Manual dexterity is essential, and good home conditions with the facility of a bathroom and toilet combined are desirable.

As this procedure can take from three-quarters of an hour to one and a quarter hours, the patient must be able to spare the time. A supportive and understanding family is important, so that sufficient time can be spent in the bathroom without frequent interruptions.

Although irrigation is not suitable for the double-barrelled transverse temporary colostomy, it can be a convenient and efficient procedure for washing through the distal and proximal loops prior to surgery for closure of colostomy. At the surgeon's request the trained ward nursing staff can irrigate the proximal loop (as explained later in this chapter). The distal loop can be washed through in the same way with the water being expelled through the rectum, with the patient sitting on a commode or the toilet. This will remove all retained faecal matter or barium prior to surgery.

EQUIPMENT REQUIRED FOR IRRIGATION

As has already been mentioned, the patient must have adquate home conditions, the ideal being a bathroom and toilet combined. The irrigation kit (Figure 11.1) constructed of a lightweight plastic consists of:

1) A reservoir/irrigator with a measuring guide on the side (the Hollister irrigation kit is marked in American pints);
2) A clear plastic tube leading from the irrigator to the cone with a flow control valve on the tube;
3) The cone (Figure 11.2), which is made of a soft plastic and constructed in such a way as to allow a leak-proof junction when placed in the stoma opening;
4) A long drain open at the top and bottom. The drain is attached to the abdomen by adhesive or a soft adjustable belt;
5) A clip that can be attached to the bottom of the drain after the initial faecal evacuation to give freedom of movement to the patient;
6) Lubricating gel to lubricate the cone before insertion into the stoma;
7) A plastic glove to wear if dilatation of the stoma is necessary;
8) A plastic hook to be situated on the wall on the left hand side of the toilet if possible, positioned so that the bottom of the irrigator is at shoulder height when the patient is sitting;

9) A jug of water to wash out the drain after use. This is simply done by leaving the drain in situ on the abdomen and flushing through with water.

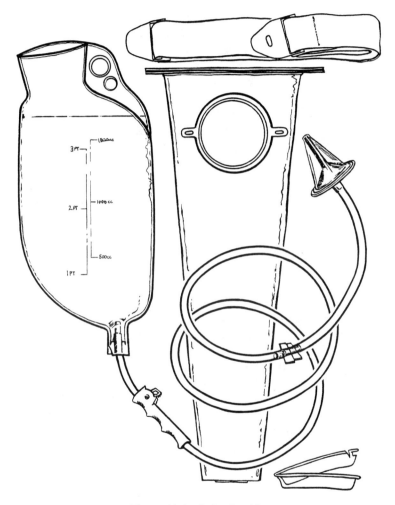

Figure 11.1   Irrigation kit.

10) A colostomy appliance, if necessary, or a lubricated piece of gauze held in place with adhesive, or a stoma cap. A stoma cap is made of non-adherent absorbent dressing with an adhesive surround; a flatus filter is incorporated.

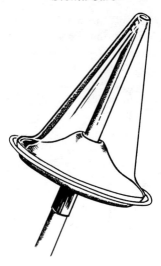

Figure 11.2   Irrigation cone.

TEACHING THE IRRIGATION TECHNIQUE

The patient must first be seen and examined by the surgeon and stoma care nurse. This is to exclude the presence of any metastatic carcinoma, and to observe the stoma to discover which way it has been fashioned, so that the cone can be introduced in the right direction. The stoma is also examined to discern whether dilation is necessary, which is the case if the stoma is narrow. This is easily detected by inserting a lubricated gloved finger gently into the stoma.

It is important that the patient is given adequate instructions by a trained nurse with specific knowledge of this procedure, preferably a stoma care nurse or ward or community sister. Detailed instructions, both verbal and written, should be given and ideally the first irrigation performed with the nurse in attendance. The importance of this cannot be stressed enough, as it can be a traumatic experience for the patient if the irrigation procedure is performed without adequate guidance.

The patient is instructed to irrigate daily for the first week, then advised to irrigate every other day to discover if it is possible to be free from a colostomy action for forty-eight hours. Some patients manage irrigation every third day, depending to a great extent on the bowel activity. The patient will soon discover what the maximum time between irrigations can be.

It is irrelevant at what time irrigation is performed, but initially it must be at approximately the same time each day. Patients who go to work or have a young family may find it convenient in the evening, while the housewife who spends her time at home may prefer mid-morning.

At the initial examination and teaching session the patient is instructed on the right amount of water to use. This varies between 1000ml and 1500ml (2–3 pints), depending on the patient's weight and size. The doctor or stoma care nurse will decide on the correct amount.

The patient should be seen one week after starting irrigation to assess results and sort out any problems that may have arisen.

The patient should be encouraged to contact the doctor, stoma care nurse or whoever has the expertise in this field, if he has any worries or problems. It is important that as much support as possible is given at this time.

METHOD OF IRRIGATION

The patient must be relaxed and unhurried, and the family instructed that the toilet will be occupied for approximately one hour and that there should be no interruptions.

1) The equipment is assembled within easy reach.
2) The irrigator is filled with luke-warm tap water, to the amount prescribed, making sure that the flow control valve is switched off. The irrigator is placed on the hook on the left hand side of the toilet. A little water is allowed into the tube to expel the air.
3) The tube is pushed to the end of the cone; if this is not done water will pool in the cone.
4) The stoma cap or appliance is removed.
5) The drain is placed over the stoma (Figure 11.3) making sure the top is open. The belt is fixed to the gasket on the drain and adjusted to make a firm snug fit.
6) The patient then sits on the toilet or on a chair facing the toilet, with the bottom of the drain in the toilet pan.
7) The lubricating gel is applied to the cone and a gloved finger inserted into the stoma, if prescribed, to dilate it. (Most patients find this very distasteful and are reluctant to do it.)
8) The cone is inserted (Figure 11.4) through the top of the drain and into the stoma, in the direction shown by the nurse. The cone is held in place by gentle pressure only.

Figure 11.3   Drainage sleeve in position over the stoma.

9) The flow control valve is opened and the water slowly enters the colon, which usually takes about ten minutes.
10) After all the water has entered the colon, the flow control valve is switched off and the cone is removed. The top of the drain is rolled down, away from the body, until securely closed, to prevent splash back.
11) After the initial return of the water and faecal content, the clip can be applied to the bottom of the drain.
12) Evacuation usually takes between a half to three-quarters of an hour. The drain can then be flushed through and removed and dried.
13) The stoma is then cleaned with soft toilet tissue or kitchen paper roll and a piece of lubricated gauze or a stoma cap is applied.
   The patient is advised to continue wearing a colostomy appliance until the technique has been completely mastered and he is confident there will be no stomal action between irrigations.

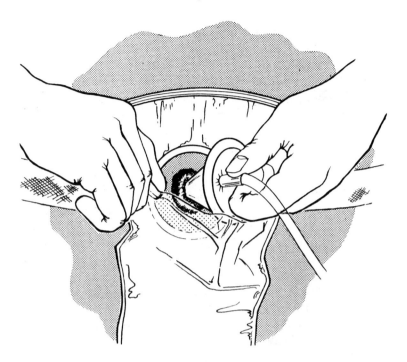

Figure 11.4   Insertion of the cone into the stoma.

OTHER CONSIDERATIONS

It is quite satisfactory to use tap water for irrigation but it must be luke-warm; hot water must never be used. If the water is too cold, abdominal cramps can occur when it is introduced. If this should happen, the flow control valve should be switched off and the cone removed from the stoma. The abdomen should be massaged gently until the cramp subsides. The water temperature should be checked and corrected if necessary. The irrigation can then be continued.

Tap water in some countries is not suitable for irrigation, as it may be contaminated with organisms which could cause gastrointestinal dysfunction or infection. Some patients have complained of abdominal pain and diarrhoea after using unsuitable water for irrigation. Patients may be advised to use bottled water, which can be easily purchased, if they are not sure of the quality of local water.

When first starting irrigation, patients must be advised to continue wearing their colostomy appliance, as has been mentioned earlier in this chapter. A supply of appliances must always be kept in case of a mild gastrointestinal infection resulting in diarrhoea. A normal diet can be taken when irrigating. It is inadvisable to drink large quantities of beer, although it may be taken in moderation. Flatus with accompanying odour and noise should abate.

The irrigation procedure can easily be adapted when away from home, either on business trips or holidays staying in a hotel, private house or camp site. Many patients who travel widely because of their employment find irrigation a very convenient way of colostomy control.

Plastic stick-on hooks can be used and placed by the toilet, or facilities that are available can be adapted, e.g. by tying some string to a window hook and suspending the irrigator from this. One patient, who is a musician, has adapted her music stand for this purpose. Patients should be reminded to take a supply of appliances in case diarrhoea occurs.

Patients should be advised to irrigate before travelling, and on arrival, and then to continue as normal, i.e. irrigating every twenty-four or forty-eight hours. The irrigation kits are very compact and take up very little space. It is advisable that the kit should be carried in the hand luggage, as suitcases can get lost.

In the United States and in some hospitals in the United Kingdom patients are taught to irrigate while still in hospital. Other centres wait until at least three months after surgery in order to assess the patient's capabilities and home conditions.

If the irrigation technique has to be discontinued because of ill-health or a change in home conditions, the colostomy action returns to normal.

Irrigation can be of great help for the patient who suffers from constipation. A mild aperient may still be necessary occasionally.

PROBLEMS

Difficulty with water not running into the colon
This can be due to the cone being positioned incorrectly, since it must follow the direction of the colon. This is easily remedied by inserting a gloved finger gently into the stoma to discern the direction in which the stoma has been fashioned, then repositioning the cone.

Difficulty in inserting the cone into the stoma
This may be due to tension or the stomal opening being narrow. Daily dilation to relax and stretch the stoma may be necessary.

Water/effluent not being expelled
This may be because the patient is very tense while irrigating. He should be encouraged to relax the abdomen by deep breathing and gentle massage. Slight activity can also help the effluent to be discharged.

Stomal action between irrigations
This is usually due to the irrigation being rushed, and by not allowing sufficient time for the water and effluent to be discharged completely. There may be other causes such as a para colostomy hernia, in which case medical advice must be sought.

Bleeding from the stoma
This may be due to trauma, e.g. the patient may be pushing the cone too hard into the stoma. Medical advice must be sought if the problem continues.

Unsatisfactory results from irrigation
A poor result with little faecal return may occasionally happen, but irrigation must not be repeated the same day. Irrigation should be satisfactory the following day.

OBTAINING AND CARING FOR EQUIPMENT

The irrigation kit can be used for approximately eighteen months to two years. The plastic tubing may become discoloured in time due to deposits in the water, but it is still safe to use. The cone may be dismantled and washed, but never in boiling water. The drains can be used for approximately two to three months, and should be washed and dried after each use. The equipment must be stored in a cool dry place away from heat and direct sunlight. The equipment should be disposed of by incineration, or wrapped up well and placed in a dustbin.

All irrigation kits are available from hospital stores, and some can be obtained on FP.10.

The irrigation technique has been used at the author's hospital for approximately three years, and it has proved to be an effective way of promoting colostomy control. Patients are enthusiastic about the results:

'No comparison in quality and refinement of life, improved one hundred per cent.'

'I feel much cleaner.'

'The routine makes life much more orderly and normal.'

'If prepared to give the time required, results are superb.'

'Holidays are fun again.'

REFERENCE

Devlin, H. B., Plant, J. A. and Griffin, M. 1971. *Brit. Med. J. 3,* 413.

QUESTIONS AND DISCUSSION

1) What is the principle of irrigation?
2) Which patients must be excluded from irrigation, and why?
3) What improvements do patients achieve through irrigation?
4) What is the approximate time after surgery before patients can commence irrigation?
5) How would you advise patients when travelling abroad or going on holiday?
6) What is the cause of stomal bleeding when irrigating, and what action should be taken?
7) What are the reasons for difficulty in inserting the cone into the stoma?
8) How could irrigation be used prior to closure of a double-barrelled transverse colostomy?
9) What facilities do patients need for irrigating?

Chapter 12

Dietary Considerations and the Use of Bran

The dietary aim following stoma surgery is to ensure that the patient resumes normal eating habits. The term diet is inappropriate, as it is important that the patient sees before him a complete return to health and normality. When the patient's choice has been severely limited as a result of his disease, he must be re-educated to adopt a wider range of foodstuffs, incorporated into wholesome, appetising and attractive meals. Such patients may benefit from a chat with the dietitian, and by being given a simple instruction sheet before they are discharged.

THE URINARY DIVERSION

CUTANEOUS URETEROSTOMY

Patients who have a cutaneous ureterostomy will be able to resume their normal eating habits once the effects of the anaesthetic and pain-relieving drugs wear off. A good fluid intake is advised.

URINARY CONDUIT

Patients with a urinary conduit frequently have problems with flatulence and resumption of normal bowel activity immediately after surgery. This is due to the slowing down or cessation of peristalsis which occurs following handling of the gut, when a piece of bowel is isolated to form the conduit and the remaining bowel is anastamosed to restore continuity.

Once paralytic ileus resolves, the patient should have bland types of food, increasing gradually to normal meals of the patient's own choice. No dietary restrictions are necessary. A good fluid intake should be encouraged, sufficient to ensure a urinary output of 1600–1800ml a day. Some authorities encourage consumption of fruit juices rich in vitamin C, such as cranberry juice, blackcurrant juice and rosehip syrup, as these substances help to produce a strongly acid urine. It is thought that this decreases the likelihood of some urinary infections and resultant odorous urine. Asparagus is known to produce strong-smelling urine in some people, but with odour-proof equipment, and the prohibitive cost of asparagus, this is unlikely to pose a problem.

The patient should be encouraged to increase his fluid consumption in very hot weather, when sweating eliminates a fair amount of body fluid. Decreased urinary output leads to a collection of mucus, secreted by the mucous membrane lining the conduit, risking a block or infection. The fluid intake should also be increased if the urine appears concentrated.

Alcohol need not be restricted, but it should be stressed that over-indulgence produces carelessness in emptying the appliance, and therefore leakage can occur.

ILEOSTOMY

The person with ulcerative colitis or Crohn's disease may have severely restricted his diet for a considerable period before surgery, in an attempt to restrict frequent bowel actions. He may be reluctant to try more varied eating habits if, in the past, different foodstuffs have been blamed for frequency of stool and abdominal discomfort. A suggestion sheet may be of help (see Table 12.1).

Effluent from the ileostomy should assume a toothpaste consistency. Medication may help to achieve this initially. A copious watery stool quickly dehydrates the ileostomist – it may herald an attack of gastroenteritis, a recurrence of inflammation in the proximal loop of a patient with Crohn's disease, or the onset of an obstruction brought about by a collection of undigested food, usually cellulose, which is not dealt with efficiently by the small bowel. The patient with a watery stool should be encouraged to increase his fluid intake, adding a small amount of salt to correct the electrolyte imbalance. Medical advice should be sought immediately. In extreme cases the patient might require intravenous therapy. Excessive flatulence and odour may be decreased by the addition of yoghurt to meals, and buttermilk if available is most helpful. These two substances also help to stem 'fluid run off', brought about by oral antibiotic therapy where the normal intestinal flora is altered.

The patient is advised to exercise caution for up to six weeks post-operatively, then to proceed as suggested in Table 12.1.

Table 12.1   Food and your ileostomy

The guidelines are designed to help you enjoy your food and keep you fit. There is no need to follow a 'special diet'. Because people are different, not all points will apply to everyone.

1) Eat as normally as possible.
2) Eat a wide variety of food. Try to include some fresh vegetables or fruit each day, e.g. potatoes, carrots, banana, orange juice.
3) Try new food in small amounts, one at a time; wait a few days before trying another new food. This is to enable you to isolate any problem food.
4) Avoid only those foods which upset *you*.
5) Be cautious about a few foods such as onions, dried fruit, peas, nuts, coconut.
6) Drink ordinary amounts of tea or other liquids. You may need more liquids in hot weather.
7) Yoghurt and buttermilk help to eliminate odour and fluid stool, as well as 'windy' problems.

Foodstuffs to be taken cautiously are those high in cellulose content, namely coconut, shells of peas, celery, popcorn and most vegetables used in Chinese meals, such as bean sprouts and bamboo shoots. The digestive enzyme necessary to break down cellulose into sugar is not contained in the human gut. This group of foods produces problems of an obstructive nature only when there is a mechanical abnormality, such as a narrowing of the neck of the stoma, adhesions, or a trapped or twisted loop of small bowel.

Oral hygiene is important and dental deficiencies should be corrected. The patient should be instructed to chew all food well, to have regular meals and not to bolt food. Fluids are better taken when eating is completed, as the digestive process is not improved by taking large quantities of fluid with meals.

Alcohol need not be restricted; excess can produce carelessness in the emptying of the appliance, as previously described for the urinary diversion patient. Some patients find that alcohol taken on an empty stomach produces over-stimulation of the gut, giving rise to excess flatulence, and in some instances an excessive amount of watery stool.

COLOSTOMY

This area will be considered in two sections, sigmoid colostomy and transverse colostomy.

SIGMOID COLOSTOMY

It is hoped that the patient with a left-sided sigmoid colostomy will resume a normal or near normal stool consistency. Sensible eating helps to achieve this in most cases soon after the operation, although this may be delayed in the presence of some medication (see Chapter 13).

As stated in Chapter 2, the colon is encouraged to void its contents as a result of the gastro-colic reflex. This occurs after main meals, particularly the first meal of the day. Some authorities encourage the patient to have two hot cups of tea immediately on rising, followed by breakfast thirty minutes later. The colostomy frequently acts quite soon after this. The appliance may then be changed; in some patients it may not require changing until bed-time, as the colostomy is less active once the normal daily volume of faeces is evacuated. A regular bowel action may be achieved as a result of regular meals. Patients who nibble snacks frequently throughout the day usually have frequent small bowel actions. A light diet, followed by the gradual inclusion of the patient's choice of food in small tempting meals at regular intervals, with the instruction to chew all food well and not to bolt it, is recommended.

Immediately post-operatively, the patient may be plagued with excessive flatulence, as his period on intravenous fluids, nil by mouth, and efficient bowel preparation pre-operatively will have ensured a completely cleared out gut. First bowel actions are usually fluid. The addition of the coarse variety of natural wheat bran to the diet, as soon as solid food is recommenced, is sometimes advocated. This helps to produce a less fluid stool. Eventually, as a result of the bulking qualities of bran, it encourages the formation of a semi-solid or formed stool at more regular intervals, instead of the constant voiding of faecal fluid. Guidelines on the amount of bran to be taken, and ways of incorporating it into a normal diet, can be given to the patient in a suggestion sheet (see Table 12.2).

Patients should be asked to experiment with the amounts of bran they take, as individual needs differ. Two teaspoonfuls should be taken twice a day initially, then two teaspoonfuls at night only for a few days, then two teaspoonfuls in the morning only, to see which amount and

---

Table 12.2 Food and your colostomy.

The guidelines are designed to help you enjoy your food and keep you fit. There is no need to follow a 'special diet'. Because people are different, not all the points will apply to everyone.
1) Eat as normally as possible.
2) Eat a wide variety of food: try to include some fresh vegetables or fruit each day, for example – potatoes, carrots, bananas, oranges or orange juice.
3) Try new foods in small amounts, one at a time; wait a few days before trying another new food. This is to enable you to isolate any problem food.
4) Avoid only those foods which upset *you*.
5) Be cautious about a few foods such as onions, dried fruit, peas and nuts.
6) Drink ordinary amounts of tea or other liquids.
7) Take two teaspoonfuls of unprocessed bran once or twice daily according to need. (This is to give a formed stool once or twice daily.) The bran can be taken with cereal, milk, yoghurt, soup or fruit juice, according to taste.
8) Yoghurt and buttermilk are most helpful in the diminution of odour and 'windy' problems.

---

which time suits the patient best. It should be stressed that the coarse type of bran is considered the most efficient. Instructions on the packets of proprietary brands of bran should be ignored, as some advocate amounts far in excess of the requirements of the colostomist. These larger quantities are not harmful, but can produce abdominal cramps, excess wind, and a large increase in the volume of faecal material voided, requiring more frequent changing of the appliance.

Ultimately the patient should be able to return to varied and attractive meals of his own choice, exercising caution at first in the amount of food introduced, and not including in any one meal more than one foodstuff which is known to stimulate bowel activity. For example, peas as a vegetable in the main course should not be followed by rhubarb tart and custard as a sweet as both peas and rhubarb stimulate bowel activity. It would be more prudent to have cheese and biscuits instead of the fruit tart on this occasion. Given a few explicit instructions, the patient will return home full of confidence and will soon find he is not even bothered by eating meals away from home, as he learns to select a balanced meal.

Beer drinkers will already be aware that this beverage can produce a fluid stool, but some patients overcome this problem by taking extra bran before they embark on their evening jollification, as they find it counteracts the effects of the beer! Too much indulgence can, as previously mentioned, lead to carelessness in handling the appliance. Bran is not obtainable on prescription. It can be purchased from any health store and some chemists, and it is extremely cheap to buy. Bran absorbs water and softens constipated stools. In diarrhoea it absorbs water and thickens the liquid, so it tends to bring the stool towards the normal consistency. The amount needed depends on the amount of fibre in the rest of the patient's diet (Painter, 1974).

Constipation is not a common problem for the patient with a sigmoid colostomy. Absence of the rectum and sphincter muscles results in free passage of mainly formed faeces, without the storage and dehydration which normally takes place in the rectum. It may occur if the patient is obliged to take pain-relieving drugs as a result of the progress of his original disease. Natural means of relieving this condition should be advocated, such as an increase in the vegetable, fruit and bran content of the diet. It may later be necessary to take a mild aperient regularly to counteract the effect of these drugs.

TRANSVERSE COLOSTOMY

The advice given to the patient with a transverse colostomy differs very little from that given to a person with a left sigmoid colostomy. The fluid state of the faecal effluent endures for a longer period, especially if the patient has had a total obstruction of the bowel. His general pre-operative condition may be impaired as a result of his illness, usually of malignant origin, although diverticular disease can be responsible for obstructive and perforated bowel conditions.

Reluctance to eat needs gentle and sympathetic handling by the nursing and dietetic staff; small tempting meals of the patient's own choice should be offered. Although electrolyte imbalance will have been corrected by intravenous therapy immediately post-operatively, a good fluid intake should be encouraged to replace the fluid loss.

Patients with transverse colostomies rarely pass formed stools, but most produce a semi-solid toothpaste consistency stool in time. Occasionally medication is required in order to expedite the correction of severe fluid loss via the colostomy (see Chapter 13).

The return to normal eating following stoma surgery is now the rule rather than the exception. In the past, low residue diets were advocated, resulting in patients suffering from extreme loss of weight in some cases, as the foodstuffs suggested were too expensive to buy. They also resulted in vitamin deficiences due to lack of fresh fruit and vegetables, and a complete change of life style due to altered eating habits. Fortunately, as a result of the combined efforts of doctors, nurses, dietitians and appliance manufacturers, those days have now passed.

REFERENCE

Painter, N. S. 1974. *Diverticular Disease of the Colon.* Norgine Ltd.

QUESTIONS FOR DISCUSSION

1) What is the dietary aim following stoma surgery?
2) Does the patient who has a urinary conduit have any gastro-intestinal dysfunction post-operatively?
3) How much urinary output should the patient with a urinary diversion aim for in twenty-four hours?
4) What could a copious watery stool passed by an ileostomy patient indicate?
5) Which foodstuffs may be added to the diet to help reduce flatulence and odour for the colostomist or ileostomist?
6) Which substance is not dealt with efficiently in the human gut? Give two sources of this substance.
7) Does alcohol need to be excluded from the diet of a patient with a stoma?
8) What is the effect of including natural wheat bran in the diet of a patient with a colostomy?
9) When is a patient with a colostomy likely to suffer from severe constipation?

Chapter 13

Medication and Stomal Action

Warrington (1979) makes two very relevant comments with reference to medication and stomal action. First, 'sooner or later patients with stomas will need treatment with a drug', and second, 'almost any drug is capable of causing disturbances in bowel function'.

In discussing drugs that affect stomal action there are two main groups. There are drugs which are prescribed to affect bowel function, for example laxatives, and drugs which are prescribed for other conditions but have an incidental action on stoma function. In this second group there are drugs that may cause constipation as a side effect, or drugs that may cause diarrhoea. Colostomists and ileostomists are on the whole much more aware of the consistency of their stool than non-ostomists, and consequently more aware of drugs causing constipation or diarrhoea. More important, a sudden change in stomal action may cause problems for the ostomist – a very loose motion may necessitate a colostomist using a drainable appliance rather than a non-drainable appliance.

CLASSIFICATION OF DRUGS WHICH AFFECT BOWEL FUNCTION

ACTION OF DRUGS VIA THE AUTONOMIC NERVOUS SYSTEM

The gastrointestinal tract is controlled by the autonomic nervous system, consisting of two parts, the sympathetic and the para-sympathetic (see Chapter 2). Parasympathetic stimulation increases activity in the gut and the sympathetic causes inhibition and slowing of the gastrointestinal activity. The chemical transmitter released at the parasympathetic nerve termination is acetylcholine, and such nerve fibres are known as cholinergic. The chemical transmitter at the sympathetic nerve termination is noradrenaline, and the nerves are said to be adrenergic. Drugs can affect stomal action through the cholinergic system or via the adrenergic system.

Cholinergic drugs
When acetylcholine is released it is rapidly destroyed by the enzyme cholinesterase. Drugs which suppress or inhibit the action of the enzymes are known as anticholinesterases. These drugs prolong the activity of acetylcholine and produce intensified effects. Included in this group are neostigmine (Prostigmin), used in the treatment of myasthenia gravis, and distigmine (Ubretid), sometimes used for treatment of neurogenic bladder. These drugs may cause diarrhoea.

Anticholinergic drugs
Many drugs inhibit the action of acetylcholine released at nerve endings, and are said to be anticholinergic. The oldest and most widely used member of this group is belladonna and the alkaloid atropine obtained from it. Atropine acts by competing for the same receptors as acetylcholine, occupying them and rendering the acetylcholine ineffectual. The general effect is a reduction of muscle tone, and peristalsis in the gastrointestinal tract. The end result may be constipation. An example of a drug containing atropine is Belladenal, which contains belladonna in combination with phenobarbitone. A large number of synthetic atropine-like compounds have been developed and include propantheline (Probanthine) and emepronium (Cetiprin), prescribed for the treatment of urinary frequency, gastrointestinal spasm and gastric acid hypersecretion.

Sympathomimetic drugs
These drugs mimic the effect of stimulation of the sympathetic nerves and may cause constipation. Examples of sympathomimetic drugs are diethylpropion (Apisate and Tenuate), which is an appetite suppressant. The monoamine oxidase inhibitors have a sympathetic stimulatory effect, which is also constipating.

Adrenergic blocking drugs
Adrenergic neurone blocking drugs act by preventing the release of the chemical transmitter noradrenaline and therefore the sympathetic effects are depressed. Guanethidine (Ismelin) and bethanidine (Esbatal) are the two principal drugs in this group used in the treatment of hypertension. The use of such drugs may result in diar-

rhoea, commonly attributed to parasympathetic predominance after sympathetic blockade.

DIRECT ACTION OF DRUGS ON THE GUT

Drugs can affect the gastrointestinal activity by direct action on the gut. Included in this group are the analgesics which cause gastrointestinal muscle spasm. Morphine acts directly on the smooth muscle of both large and small bowel causing it to contract. The normal propulsive action is markedly reduced, resulting in constipation.

INDIRECT ACTION OF DRUGS ON THE GUT

The action of the third group of drugs which may affect the gut is difficult to explain, because their effects are mediated through other systems. A diuretic may affect the function of the gut by acting both directly on the sodium potassium balance across the intestinal smooth muscle cell membrane, and also by reducing the extracellular fluid volume, resulting in increased water absorption from the stool in the large bowel.

DRUGS WHICH ARE GIVEN TO CONTROL STOMAL ACTION

LAXATIVES

The terms purgative, laxative, aperient and evacuant are synonymous, and are usually classified as bulk, lubricant or irritant laxatives.

Bulk laxatives
These act by increasing the volume of intestinal contents and so encourage normal reflex bowel activity. These are two main groups. The hydrophilic colloids absorb water and promote a soft solid stool. Methylcellulose (Celevac) and a preparation of ispaghula husk BPC (Isogel) work in this way and are prescribed for the colostomist to help him to obtain a more formed stool. Inorganic salts increase the bulk of intestinal contents by an osmotic effect, retaining water in the intestinal lumen; or, if given in a hypertonic solution, by withdrawing it from the body. The principal substances used as purgatives are magnesium sulphate (Epsom Salts) and sodium sulphate (Glauber's Salt).

Irritant laxatives

These drugs contain anthraquinones which cause a mild irritation of the intestine, thus increasing the rate of peristalsis. It is thought that they stimulate Auerbach's Plexus in the large intestine. Included in this group are cascara, senna and danthron, which is a synthetic anthraquinone. This is used in combination with Poloxamer (which increases the penetration of water into the faecal mass) in the drug Dorbanex and Dorbanex Forte, which is often prescribed for drug-induced constipation.

Lubricant laxatives

Liquid paraffin, a mineral oil, is the only important example of this group. It is thought to act by lubricating the bowel. It is not often used alone but given in an emulsion together with magnesium hydroxide (Milpar).

BLOCKERS

Both colostomists and ileostomists, like non-ostomists, are at risk of developing a 'bowel upset' and having diarrhoea, and may require medication to control their symptoms. For the person without a stoma one to two days of diarrhoea are not usually too troublesome, and apart from the inconvenience of frequent visits to the toilet, they are able to tolerate the physiological complications. For the ileostomist with diarrhoea the problems are twofold. First, because he has no colon to exert the normal regulatory function over water and electrolyte balance, he is at greater risk of becoming dehydrated. Secondly, a very high output may cause problems with the appliance, and in very severe cases it is sometimes impossible for the patient to secure an appliance. For the colostomist the problem of dehydration is not as dangerous. But, as already discussed earlier, an attack of diarrhoea may necessitate the patient changing his appliance from a non-drainable to a drainable type. In addition he may require some added skin protection, as used by the ileostomist.

Ileostomists who have had part of the small bowel resected, or who have active Crohn's disease, may persistently have a high output fluid stool, and may need a regular dose of a constipating agent. If a colostomist has a very fluid stool, causing management problems, he too may need a constipating agent to help him obtain a more formed stool.

Drugs used in the control of diarrhoea are often used in combination.

Adsorbents
Adsorbent powders are thought to be able to absorb toxic gases and to provide a coating for the bowel. Although neither explanation is entirely satisfactory these agents appear to work. Preparations include kaolin compound BPC and kaolin and morphine mixture BPC, in which the kaolin is combined with an opiate.

Opiate derivatives
More effective than the adsorbent powders is the opiate group of drugs which act directly on the smooth muscle of the bowel, with morphine as the classical example. The drugs commonly used for the treatment of diarrhoea are codeine (codeine phosphate) and diphenoxylate, which is chemically related to pethidine but is a much more effective anti-diarrhoea agent than pethidine. It is found in the preparation Lomotil, where it is combined with a small dose of atropine.

More potent than Lomotil is a new drug loperamide (Imodium), which has been found to be very effective in the treatment of both diarrhoea and high ileostomy output. It inhibits peristaltic activity by interacting with cholinergic as well as non-cholinergic neuronal mechanisms.

MANAGEMENT OF MEDICATION BY THE OSTOMIST

Celevac and Isogel can be used for the treatment of constipation. They can also be used to help the colostomy patient obtain a more formed stool. A colostomist may complain that his stoma works many times throughout the day, but that he only passes a very small stool each time it acts. If mechanical causes, for example stenosis, have been eliminated, and if the use of bran (see Chapter 12) does not help, then Celevac or one of the bulking agents should be tried. It should be taken in a small amount of fluid, and ideally the patient should have nothing to drink half an hour before and half an hour afterwards. It is important that the patient understands this, because otherwise he may follow the instructions on the package for its use in the treatment of constipation, where it is taken in a glass of fluid. This results in the patient having a very fluid stool, which is probably more troublesome than his original complaint. Patients find that it is more palatable if taken in a carbonated drink, but there are still many patients who find it difficult to swallow. The recommended dosage is one to two level 5ml teaspoonfuls of granules twice daily. However, patients need to adjust the dosage to produce motions of the desired consistency.

The colostomy patient with cancer may ultimately develop pain and will require analgesics, which may produce constipation. In these circumstances it is often necessary for him to have a laxative prescribed routinely. Each patient, as always, is an individual, and the choice of laxative will depend on many factors, including the doctor's personal preference.

Patients undergoing radiotherapy and antitumour chemotherapy may have altered bowel action and may suffer from diarrhoea and constipation, which may require medication (see Chapter 14).

DRUGS WHICH MAY BE PRESCRIBED AND WHICH HAVE AN EFFECT ON STOMAL ACTION

One factor which is apparent in dealing with drugs is the variation in patients' reactions to them. This is true not only of ostomists but of non-ostomists. It is worth telling ostomists that any drug may alter their bowel activity, but that this is expected and is quite normal. Unless it causes management problems they should continue taking the drug.

CONSTIPATORS

Any drug with anticholinergic effects causes constipation. An important group with anticholinergic effects is the tricyclic antidepressants, such as amitriptyline (Tryptizol), dothiepin (Prothiaden) and imipramine (Tofranil). If colostomists and ileostomists suffer from depression they may have one of the tricyclic antidepressants prescribed for them. If constipation becomes a problem laxatives may be necessary.

Drugs used in the treatment of Parkinsonism are anticholinergic and are constipating. Examples are benzhexol (Artane), benztropine (Cogentin) and orphenadrine (Disipal).

The phenothiazine group of tranquillisers, for example chlorpromazine (Largactil), also have an anticholinergic effect and may cause constipation.

Chlorpromazine (Largactil) potentiates the action of analgesics, and may be prescribed in conjunction with an analgesic for the terminal patient. A colostomist receiving one of the narcotic analgesics and Largactil may become very constipated unless a laxative is prescribed. Antihistamines, such as chlorpheniramine (Piriton) and cyproheptadine (Periactin), have an anticholinergic effect and may be constipating in combination with other anticholinergic drugs. Other drugs which may constipate as a side effect are narcotic derivatives, for example codeine and dextro-propoxyphene (Distalgesic).

In comparison with the magnesium based antacids, which cause diarrhoea, the aluminium and calcium based antacids are constipating. If an ostomist requires an antacid, it may be necessary to prescribe either one of the magnesium antacids or a calcium/aluminium antacid, depending on the stool. Sometimes a combination of both may achieve the required stool consistency.

LAXATIVES

Just as troublesome as the drugs that cause constipation are those causing diarrhoea, such as antibiotics. It is thought that antibiotics alter the normal intestinal flora and this may result in diarrhoea. Ampicillin and the tetracyclines are common offenders and it is useful to warn the patient that diarrhoea may occur when taking these, but he should not be discouraged from taking them.

DRUGS AND NON-ABSORPTION IN THE GUT

Most drugs are readily absorbed from the mucosal surface of the gastrointestinal tract. The amount of drug absorbed after oral administration may vary, because of the variations in the rate of passage through the stomach and intestine. If a patient has a rapid transit time, either because of disease or previous surgery, he may not always fully absorb the drug.

Some tablets consists of a wax matrix containing the active drug which is slowly released during passage through the gut. The empty matrix is excreted intact in the stool. Although this is not peculiar to ostomists they are more likely to notice it in their bag, and may think they are not absorbing any of the drug. Examples of such tablets are Slow K, Slow Fe, Navidrex K and Ferrogradumet. A simple explanation prior to prescribing such drugs for ostomists will help. Some female ileostomists have noticed that their contraceptive pill has been excreted in their faeces. Although there is no evidence of this in the literature, the occurrence would be explained if part of the small bowel has been resected. If patients notice their pill in the bag, and if they are having any signs of break-through bleeding, they are probably not having full contraceptive protection and should seek advice about alternative methods of contraception. Low dose oral contraceptives are probably unsuitable for these patients.

DISCOLOURATION OF URINE AND FAECES

A considerable number of drugs discolour the urine, faeces or both. Although this is not peculiar to stoma patients, they may be more likely to notice the change in colour, and this can cause unnecessary anxiety. Examples of drugs that colour the urine are amitryptiline (blue/green), riboflavin (deep yellow), phenytoin (Epanutin) (pink/brown). Drugs containing ferrous salts will make the stool black, as will bismuth-containing preparations.

Patients with stomas are no more likely to suffer drug side effects than patients without. It is important that patients understand this, so that they are not afraid of taking medication. Some ostomists have grave misconceptions about their stoma, and may even be afraid to take two soluble aspirins for headache for fear of upsetting it. Patients must be told that almost any drug may affect bowel function, but that they as ostomists will probably be more aware of any effects. It is also important that patients understand they are not immune to diarrhoea and constipation, and may require the appropriate treatment.

REFERENCE

Warrington, Steven 1979. *Pharmacological Considerations,* Rcn Stoma Care Nursing Forum. Abbott Laboratories Limited, November.

QUESTIONS FOR DISCUSSION

1) Explain briefly how cholinergic drugs act.
2) a) What is atropine? b) How does atropine act on the gut? c) What effect does it have?
3) List three types of laxatives and describe briefly how each works.
4) What drugs can be used to control ileostomy diarrhoea?

5) a) What is Celevac? b) How does it work? c) What instructions would you give to a colostomist who was prescribed Celevac to help control his colostomy?

6) What general advice would you give an ileostomist about tablet taking?

Chapter 14

The Care of the Ostomist Undergoing Radiotherapy or Antitumour Chemotherapy

The patient with a stoma coming for radiotherapy or chemotherapy will, like any other patient, need an explanation about the type of treatment he is to have, how it will be given, and any side effects which may occur during or after treatment. In addition to this general information, he will require information on any extra side effects likely to occur *because* he has a stoma.

It can thus be seen that the nurse caring for such patients will require knowledge not only of the nature of radiotherapy and chemotherapy treatment, but also of side effects of such treatments and how to deal with them most effectively.

The nature and rationale of radiotherapy and antitumour chemotherapy can best be understood in conjunction with consideration of the reproductive cycle of normal and cancer cells. Most tissues undergo this process to replace old cells, although some cells, such as those in the brain, cannot be replaced.

THE CELL CYCLE

This is a four stage process. In order to divide, a cell must be able to synthesise twice the normal amount of deoxyribonucleic acid (DNA) in its nucleus, so that its division results in two cells, each with the normal amount of DNA.

Mitosis is the process of division of one cell into two cells.

G1 is a resting phase, which follows after the cell has divided.

S phase occurs when DNA synthesis takes place, resulting in the amount of DNA in the cell being doubled.

G2 is a second resting phase, which occurs before the cell divides.

Not all the cells in any tissue are involved in this cycle of repro-duction. Those that are involved are known as the *growth fraction.* Cells which are out of cycle, or not involved, may do one of two things:
1) They may remain out of cycle and eventually die;
2) They may remain alive and eventually begin cycling again.

In normal tissues, cell division is a response to the need for replacement of cells that have died and, through control mechanisms, the number of replacement cells balances the number of destroyed cells.

In cancer cells, the control mechanisms are faulty, and uncontrolled growth occurs.

Both anti-cancer chemotherapy and radiotherapy act on normal as well as cancerous tissue. The way in which they act will be considered separately, together with the resultant side effects and the relevant nursing care for ostomists.

CHEMOTHERAPY

Cells which are in cycle are thought to be more sensitive to cytotoxic ('cell poisoning') drugs than cells which are out of cycle. It can thus be seen that normal cells in tissues such as the bone marrow, the cells of the scalp hair follicles, and the lining of the gastrointestinal tract, where a high proportion of cells are cycling, are likely to be damaged by cytotoxic drugs given to interfere with cycling abnormal or cancer cells.

Normal cells recover more rapidly than cancer cells, and a fine balance of timing of treatments must be achieved to maximise malignant cell destruction and minimise normal cell damage. This involves consideration of:
1) Whether one or more cytotoxic drugs should be used;
2) How many hours each course of chemotherapy should last;
3) What proportion of the tumour cells may be destroyed with each course;
4) How many courses the patient should have.
It has been found that some cytotoxic drugs act on cells in specific phases of the cycle. Combinations of drugs acting on different phases of the cycle can be useful in eradicating more tumour cells in radical treatment, although single agents may be used palliatively.

It has also been found that drugs given in adequate dosage over a

24–36 hour period (i.e. 1–2 cell cycles) are likely to be more effective against malignant cells, with less damage of normal cells, than drugs given over a longer period.

The concept of *fractional cell kill* has been developed from studies with animals and the results are thought to be applicable to treatment of cancers in humans. It has been established that certain cytotoxic drugs, when given to treat specific histological types of tumour, kill a fixed proportion of tumour cells, regardless of the size of the tumour.

For example: if the fixed proportion of cells which will be killed is 75 per cent, then in a tumour with 1000 cells 750 cells will be killed, and only 250 remain to start growing again; but in a tumour with 10,000 cells although 7500 cells will be killed, 2500 will remain. It can be seen it is more effective to treat tumours when they are small.

While the bulk of a tumour may be fairly easily eradicated, the small amount remaining must be treated regularly, to reduce it by the same fraction each treatment, until all the malignant cells have been eradicated. It should be remembered that cells which have remained alive but out of cycle may begin cycling again, and these cells also need to be destroyed to produce an effective cure of the disease.

If an assumption is made that the response rate is regular, an estimate of the number of courses necessary for each patient can be made.

The length of time between each course of chemotherapy will be calculated to allow recovery of normal tissue, with only partial recovery of malignant tissue. The difference in recovery is largely possible because a good proportion of normal cells are resting, and thus less vulnerable to damage from the cytotoxic drugs than the high proportion of cycling malignant cells.

With this background knowledge, the informed nurse can support the patient, explaining in terms appropriate to each individual why it is important that the treatment is given in this way, and why he should complete the required number of treatment sessions, even though troublesome symptoms may disappear before the end of the course.

Some cytotoxic drugs have side effects and the nurse should familiarise herself with those for drugs actually being given to her patients. Drug regimes change, or are modified in the light of new knowledge, and the nurse should not generalise that regimes given to the ostomist who has, for example, rectal, bladder or ovarian cancer, always cause a certain set of symptoms. It is, however, helpful if the nurse is aware of the symptoms which may arise and what measures can be taken to alleviate them.

An outline of side effects pertinent to the care of the ostomist is given here, rather than a general outline of all side effects from chemotherapeutic regimes.

GENERAL SIDE EFFECTS

Bone marrow depression

Many of the cytotoxic drugs affect the bone marrow. This may result in a fall in the number of white blood cells (leucopenia), a lowered platelet count (thrombocytopenia) and a fall in red blood cells, leading to anaemia.

Apart from the general effects resultant from bone marrow depression, such as increased susceptibility to infection and increased lethargy, the ostomist may find his stoma bleeds more readily when being cleaned. In more severe anaemia, the stoma itself may look more pallid. Such symptoms should be reported to the doctor, who may wish to check the blood count, and the patient should be reassured that there is nothing wrong with the stoma itself.

Alopecia

Patients should be informed before treatment commences if the drugs to be used may cause loss of hair. Each patient should be measured for a wig in the style of his or her choice ensuring that, if hair loss does occur, the wig is available for immediate use, helping to minimise the psychological trauma both men and women feel over this additional change in their normal body image.

Patients may be reassured that their hair will grow again at the end of their treatment, and may even have started to grow again before treatment is completed.

Cystitis

Some cytotoxic agents are excreted through the urinary system and a chemical cystitis may develop, caused by the proximity of the drugs to the bladder mucosa. This can be very painful.

It is helpful if the patient can start taking extra fluids on awakening, so that he is well hydrated before his treatment commences.

Drugs which may cause cystitis should be given *early* in the day, when the patient is awake and can be encouraged to maintain a high fluid intake to flush the drugs through his system.

Peripheral neuritis

This may occur as a result of some cytotoxic drugs, and the patient may report a tingling in the fingers and less sensitivity in handling his stoma appliance. This must be reported promptly to the medical staff, as the condition can be progressive if it is not treated.

SIDE EFFECTS WHICH MAY AFFECT STOMAL ACTION

It must be remembered that altered stomal action does not in itself automatically bring problems which the ostomist and his nurse will perceive. This is particularly true for the patient with a urinary stoma, whose diminished dietary intake may lead to a diminished urinary output. The same observation for signs of dehydration or electrolyte imbalance, which the nurse makes on patients with the more readily perceived alteration in bowel stomal output, must be maintained for the urostomist.

Mouth ulceration

This can be caused by some cytotoxic drugs, and the nurse must encourage patients to maintain a high standard of mouth care. Symptoms of dryness or increased sensitivity to hot or cold food must be reported to the doctor promptly, so that measures may be taken to minimise the ulceration and discomfort.

It may be more realistic to plan a soft or fluid diet, high in protein to encourage the recovery of normal cells, than to expect the patient to eat a normal diet. This is likely to lead to a more fluid stomal action for the colostomist or ileostomist.

Anorexia, nausea and vomiting

These side effects occur with many anti-tumour drugs. They may be the result of the drugs acting as an irritant of the stomach or duodenum, or the drugs may stimulate the vomiting centre in the brain. Antiemetics are often given routinely with cytotoxic drugs, to minimise these distressing side effects.

While nausea and vomiting may be temporary side effects present during the period of treatment, it must be remembered that some patients, particularly those taking oral anti-tumour drugs, may be nauseated and unable to eat properly over a prolonged period.

Changed dietary intake is again likely to result in altered bowel stomal output. Measures for dealing with problems arising from this will be dealt with later, in the section on radiotherapy.

Altered bowel output

Diarrhoea sometimes occurs with certain cytotoxic drugs, and can be severe. This can cause problems for the stoma patient, particularly for the colostomist who is not used to wearing a bag, or who wears a small closed style of bag.

Medication to combat more persistent diarrhoea may be necessary. It should be remembered that the patient may also be nauseated, and small tablets, such as codeine phosphate or loperamide hydrochloride (Imodium) may be more manageable than granules.

The style or size of bag a patient is wearing may need to be changed: some patients find it helpful to change to a larger capacity, drainable appliance, with a firm adhesive, for the period of their treatment. This has the added advantage of being able to be emptied with the minimum of disturbance for a weary or nauseated patient.

Constipation may occur where cytotoxic agents interfere with the function of the autonomic nervous system supplying portions of the gut, resulting in less peristalsis, and in severe cases faecal impaction, leading to paralytic ileus. Prophylactic mild aperients may be necessary. The constipation normally arises in the upper part of the colon and may not be felt on digital examination of a sigmoid colostomy.

NURSING CARE

The ostomist will require the same basic nursing care that any patient receiving chemotherapy needs, but with some important additions. *Physical care* will include mouth care, pressure-area care and blanket baths, or face and hand washes as necessary. Aids to prevent or reduce nausea, such as antiemetics, careful well-supported positioning of the patient in bed to encourage relaxation, and avoidance of subjecting the patient to smells of cooking or unpleasant odours are important. Care in presenting palatable drinks or small portioned meals is helpful.

Ostomists whose chemotherapy is given by intravenous infusion will require help emptying or changing their bags while the infusion is in progress, as well as before and after treatment, if they are nauseated or drowsy from sedatives. It can be difficult for ostomists to believe that nurses are both willing and able to carry out their stoma care, and the nurse should try to follow the patient's own routine if possible.

Changes in appliance needs while chemotherapy is being given must be discussed with each individual patient, and agreement reached over how those needs are best met, rather than changing from a familiar appliance to an unfamiliar one at a time when the patient is under stress. Considerations in this area have already been outlined in the section on diarrhoea.

Observation of the patient who is having chemotherapy should start with the nurse making herself familiar with the patient's normal habits and abilities. The nurse who knows her patient's normal eating and elimination patterns is more likely to observe departures from the normal, and be able to discuss ways of minimising problems with the patient. It is important that the patient understands *why* he is given medication or told he should drink plenty, or take a high protein diet. He must also be aware *how* and *when* to take medication. This will be discussed in more detail in the section on radiotherapy.

PSYCHOLOGICAL CARE

The ostomist will already have had one change in body image when he underwent stoma surgery. Where the stoma surgery was palliative, or where chemotherapy is being given as an adjuvant to surgery, there may have been little time for him to come to terms with his changed body image before he comes for chemotherapy treatment.

It is important that nurses realise that acceptance of hair loss, for the patient who has not had time to accept his image with a stoma, may be more difficult than for the patient without a stoma. The two together may mean that the patient takes longer to come to terms with having a stoma, as well as to losing his hair. Much support may be necessary for the patient to believe he is an acceptable human being, both to himself and to others.

Psychological vomiting by patients before they even arrive at the hospital is not uncommon, and can cause patient and family much distress. A mild tranquilliser taken for 24–48 hours before admission may be helpful.

It must be remembered that such patients may be dehydrated on arrival for treatment. This may need correction before cytotoxic drugs which must be given to a well hydrated patient can be administered.

In common with other patients receiving chemotherapy, the ostomist may find it increasingly difficult to come for each treatment, particularly if he is having unpleasant side effects. Support and encouragement, plus repeated explanations of why it is important to complete the treatment, may be needed at intervals. The patient should be encouraged to discuss his problems; nurse and patient can then work together to overcome or minimise them.

RADIOTHERAPY

A number of different ways of giving radiotherapy are available through the use of various sources. These include *interstitial therapy,* using small wires or needles; *external application,* where a source is fitted to the patient for each treatment, using a mould; the use of *liquid* radioactive material, by injection into a cavity or by selective uptake in an organ such as the thyroid; *intracavity therapy* using solid sources for areas such as the cervix and uterus, and *external beam* or *teletherapy.*

Most ostomists having radiotherapy, whether it is curative, palliative or adjuvant therapy, have external beam or *teletherapy.* It is this type of radiotherapy which will be discussed here.

Radiation is thought to be most effective in destroying cells which are cycling. The radiation which is absorbed by tissues deposits energy within them. Expenditure of that energy produces a series of chemical changes within the cell molecules, which result in cell damage. This damage is most likely to occur during the mitotic phase of the cycle or during the G2 phase, when the amount of DNA is double. The amount of damage is variable, including temporary cessation of mitotic activity, production of chromosomal abnormalities leading to cell mutations and cell death.

Cells which are primitive, undifferentiated and rapidly dividing are more radio-sensitive, or easily damaged, than well differentiated cells and cells which are slow growing.

The *method* of giving external beam therapy is based on a number of factors. The prime consideration is to focus the beam of radiation accurately on the tumour, to achieve maximum tumour destruction with minimal damage to surrounding normal tissue, and avoidance of dosage to vital structures such as the kidneys. To achieve this, a suitable source of irradiation must be chosen, which will provide penetration of the beam to the required depth of tissue. An X-ray unit, such as the linear accelerator or a gamma ray unit, such as the cobalt, may be used.

The *dosage* required will also depend on a number of factors. These include:
1) the histological type of tumour, as a more radio-sensitive tumour will require a lower dosage than a less radio-sensitive one;
2) whether the tumour is a primary or metastatic tumour;
3) whether the aim of the treatment is cure or palliation;
4) consideration of the normal tissues surrounding the tumour and their tolerance to radiation;

5) the age and general condition of the patient.

The total dose prescribed will be given by using beams in one or more fields, to reach the tumour as effectively as possible while sparing normal tissue.

The total dose will be given to the patient in *fractions*. Although this allows for recovery of tumour cells as well as normal cells between fractions, and a larger dose of radiation must be given, the recovery rate of normal tissue is quicker than that of malignant tissue and thus damage to normal tissue is minimised.

PREPARATION FOR TREATMENT

Before radiotherapy is given, a number of investigations will be carried out, including scans, X-rays and blood tests. It is important that a full picture of the patient's disease – its location, extent and any metastases – is established, as spread of the disease may mean altering the field of radiotherapy, or considering alternative treatment.

Establishment of the exact area to be treated will be carried out using a *simulator*. This establishes the length, width and depth of the tumour. It relates the tumour to reference marks on the patient's body and can reproduce the field sizes of the therapy unit.

The number of treatment fields, and their size and position, will be established through the use of a *treatment plan*. This shows the tumour and also vital areas which must receive as low a dose of radiation as possible, plus the number of fields to be used, their size and angulation. Isodose charts are used to establish the combined dosage received by tumour and normal tissue from multiple fields.

Lastly, the treatment plan must be transferred to the patient's body, by use of tattoo marks, or skin marks with indelible ink, and a check film taken of all the treatment fields with the patient lying in the treatment position. In this way, precisely the right dose to the correct area can be achieved at each treatment.

Side effects from radiotherapy vary depending on the area treated, the dose given and the degree of involvement of normal tissues. Some side effects occur at the time of treatment only, while others are long term or may manifest themselves at a later date. Indeed, on occasion, patients who have required radiotherapy to cure gynaecological or bladder tumours may later require a diversionary stoma, because of side effects such as markedly reduced bladder capacity, rectal fibrosis or stricture, or recto-vaginal or vesico-vaginal fistulae. Such sequelae are fortunately rare.

Side effects which are more likely to occur in the ostomist are discussed here.

Bone marrow depression
This can be caused by radiation if large areas of bone, such as the spine or iliac crests are being irradiated. Weekly blood counts are necessary, so that early warning of possible anaemia, leucopenia and thrombocytopenia is obtained. Side effects which the ostomist may notice have been discussed in the section on bone marrow depression due to chemotherapy.

Nausea, vomiting and anorexia
Contrary to popular belief, this does not occur with all patients receiving radiotherapy and is treatable if it does occur. Nausea may be the result of raised uric acid levels in the blood, caused by rapid tumour breakdown, or other biochemical imbalances in the blood. The position of the tumour itself, or unavoidable involvement of the gastrointestinal tract in the treatment areas of the mediastinum, abdomen and pelvis can all give rise to a patient who is nauseated and who may also have abdominal discomfort.

Altered intake will alter the stomal output. It must be remembered that radical radiotherapy treatment may be given over a six-week period, and thus problems arising from nausea or the resultant altered output can seem never-ending to the patient.

Skin problems
Skin and hair will be affected locally, both at the treatment site and at the exit point of the beam. This may not cause problems, even if the skin becomes discoloured. Patients who have a sensitive skin may have a reaction similar to sunburn. The three stages of skin reaction are:
1) *Erythema,* which is a reddening of the skin and can usually be effectively treated with calamine and tannic acid lotion;
2) *Dry desquamation* occurring with flaking of superficial layers of the skin. Calamine and tannic acid lotion continues to be useful treatment for this reaction.

3) *Moist desquamation* due to shedding of the surface epithelium. The moist area can be treated effectively with gentian violet or a steroid cream, such as betamethasone valerate (Betnovate). A non-adhesive dressing should be used and radiotherapy to the area may need to be postponed until healing has taken place.

Many ostomists find their stoma is not situated within the treatment area and therefore the skin problems outlined above do not cause stoma problems.

For those ostomists whose stoma *is* included in the treatment area, a number of considerations must be taken into account. The stoma itself will be protected with a lead shield during treatment.

Skin sparing technique
Mega voltage machines, such as the linear accelerator and sources such as the cobalt-60, operate in such a way that the maximum dosage occurs *below* the skin surface. The depth below varies from 0.5cm for the cobalt unit to 2cm for the linear accelerator. This action can be altered if a thick appliance is being worn within the treatment area, as the area with that thickness will have the depth at which maximum dose would normally occur reduced by that thickness. This can result in the irradiation beginning at the skin surface and not beneath it. Any metal, such as zinc oxide plasters or metal rings for belts, will also reduce the skin sparing effect (see Figures 14.1 and 14.2).

It can thus be seen that if the stoma and appliance come within the treatment area, a slim appliance with a non-metallic adhesive must be used. Further discussion of this point is included in the nursing care section.

Altered elimination patterns
Pelvic irradiation increases bladder irritability, and the ostomist with a bowel diversion may find himself with urinary frequency, nocturia, dysuria and may be more susceptible to infection.

Inclusion of bowel within the area of treatment for bladder, uterine or ovarian cancer, can result in diarrhoea and this can be quite severe. Treatment should be based here on a number of factors and is thus discussed within the nursing care section.

Elimination patterns may be altered as a result of radiotherapy affecting others parts of the alimentary tract. Radiotherapy to the palate or salivary glands may result in a dry mouth and loss of taste; radiotherapy to the pharynx or oesophagus may cause temporary

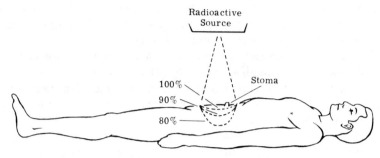

Figure 14.1   Depth below skin at which radiotherapy acts.

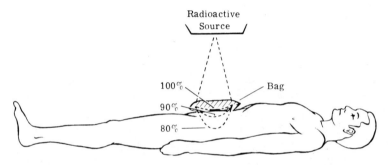

Figure 14.2   A bag containing metal applied to the skin results in radiation of tissue at less depth than planned.

oedema, and the discomfort may increase curtailment of an adequate diet, bringing altered output in its wake.

NURSING CARE

It can be seen that many of the problems which may arise for the ostomist receiving radiotherapy are interrelated. It is essential that both physical and psychological care are planned and given with an overall picture of the individual patient in mind.

Physical care
Careful monitoring of problem areas is essential if any problems which may arise are to be effectively dealt with at an early stage.
    A common complaint of bags not adhering properly may be due to

skin problems, diarrhoea, extreme weariness from nausea, a low blood count, or struggling with daily travel to and from the hospital for treatment, resulting in less efficient bag changes.

Pain is not an uncommon factor in the patient's overall picture and is almost always controllable. Patients who have been told that radiotherapy is to relieve pain often refuse analgesics, because they think the radiotherapy will be immediately effective. Careful explanation and suitable analgesics given regularly are usually necessary for some time before the effect of radiotherapy is appreciated.

The patient who is nauseated may refuse analgesics as well as diet, and will also probably have difficulty in taking medication to control diarrhoea. All medication must be given to the patient in a form which is palatable for that individual. Small pills or liquid medicines are usually more easily swallowed and retained. A nauseated patient with a loose bowel action and pain may require the following pattern of medication:

1) 30 minutes *before* meals and *before* radiotherapy treatment – anti-emetic of choice to be given;
2) 20 minutes *before* meals – a bulking agent such as codeine phosphate, alone or with an agent to slow down gut motility such as loperamide hydrochloride (Imodium) or diphenoxylate hydrochloride (Lomotil), to be given;
3) Small meals or fluids with different 'tastes' to be taken three hourly;
4) Analgesics to be taken on a *regular* basis (most have 3–4 hour period of action), in conjunction with the above timetable. Patients may find it easiest to take their analgesics during or after meals, and this is also true of antibiotics.

It is not realistic to expect patients to gain much nourishment from their food if the agents mentioned in 2) above are given after the food.

Care of the stoma requires some thought and discussion with the patient. Removal of a bulky bag or one containing a metallic adhesive brings little peace of mind to the patient anxiously awaiting an eruption of urine or faeces as he lies on the machine, having his daily treatment.

The patient whose normal appliance lies within the treatment area may have to change to a slim appliance with a non-metallic adhesive. The patient with a bowel stoma may prefer to wear a drainable bag with the larger size, reduced number of changes, and ease of emptying that this brings.

Extra skin protection may be needed and agents with only traces of metal, such as Stomahesive or karaya, are useful. Gentian violet or

Betnovate cream can be used sparingly underneath these agents on areas of moist desquamation, while still allowing adequate bag adherence to the skin.

It should not be forgotten that patients changed on to a different type of bag will need to be taught how to manage it. The patient who has pain or nausea, or is weary, will not learn easily and may need support and instruction for several changes. It is particularly helpful for the out-patient if someone in the family is able and willing to assist with bag changes, and for the in-patient if his nurse offers informed help during this period.

Most authorities agree that perfumed soaps, powders and ointments should not be used within the treatment area, because many of them contain a zinc or lead base. A plain soap with warm water is normally satisfactory for cleaning the peristomal area gently, and dabbing dry rather than too enthusiastic rubbing should be encouraged.

Psychological care
Many patients believe that all forms of radiotherapy make them radioactive. The patient who has not understood that staff must be protected from the radiation delivered to all the patients in their care, whereas he is to receive the correct dose for himself, will not be reassured by seeing staff vanishing from the room while his treatment is given.

An informed explanation tailored to a suitable level for each individual patient should be given by the ward or out-patient nurse. This will be repeated by the staff in the simulator room, and again by the radiographer manipulating the machine. This repeated information aids acceptance and lessens anxiety for most patients.

Both patient and relatives will need particular support if he is unable to tolerate their home cooking during treatment. Tactful discussion of the possibility of providing nourishing soups, jellies, egg custards and milk dishes helps the family feel more confident of their ability to support the patient, and helps the patient look forward to sampling what they provide, instead of dreading meal times.

Discussion of problems with a nurse who can listen, as well as advise, does much to minimise the depression that many patients feel at some stage during their treatment. This is particularly true if the ostomist is helped to make his own informed decisions about diet and stoma care, rather than have changes in either forced upon him. Reassurance that in time he will be able to eat normally and return to his usual bag can and should be given.

It must be remembered that an informed nurse and an informed patient can overcome many problems arising from radiotherapy and chemotherapy, if there is trust and a willingness to work together. In the past, both treatments have been seen to offer palliation alone. It is now recognised that used singly or in combination, as curative, palliative or adjuvant therapy, both radiotherapy and chemotherapy join surgery as powerful weapons in the fight against cancer.

REFERENCES

Tiffany, Robert (ed.) 1978. *Oncology for Nurses and Health Care Professionals.* Allen & Unwin.
Tiffany, Robert (ed.) 1978. *Cancer Nursing: Medical.* Faber & Faber.
Tiffany, Robert (ed.) 1979. *Cancer Nursing: Radiotherapy.* Faber & Faber.

QUESTIONS FOR DISCUSSION

The following items are included to help you check on your understanding of the material presented in this chapter. Please read each question carefully. If you are unsure of your answer, go back to the text and reread the appropriate section, where the answer can be found.

1) List the stages of the cell cycle, describing briefly what occurs at each stage.

2) Which cells are thought to be more sensitive to a) radiotherapy treatment? b) chemotherapy treatment? Give three examples for each type of treatment.

3) List four examples of general side effects which may arise from chemotherapy. Give examples for two of those side effects of symptoms which a patient might report.

4) List five side effects of chemotherapy which may affect stomal action, stating briefly how each affects stomal action.

5) What type of radiotherapy treatment is normally used for ostomists?

6) List five factors which will be considered when deciding on the dose of radiotherapy treatment for each patient.

7) List the stages of skin reaction which may arise from radiotherapy treatment, describing each stage briefly.

8) What is the skin sparing technique?

9) Give three examples of ways in which a stomal appliance situated within the area of radiotherapy treatment can alter the skin sparing mode of treatment.

10) Give two causes of nausea or vomiting in patients receiving a) chemotherapy; b) radiotherapy.

11) Discuss the pattern of care for an ostomist receiving radiotherapy who has nausea, pain, and diarrhoea. Give a brief outline of why the care you suggest is suitable.

12) Where the stoma is situated within the radiotherapy treatment area: a) What method of cleansing the area should be suggested? b) What agents should not be used and why? c) Outline briefly three ways in which extra skin protection may be given.

Chapter 15

Problems in Stoma Management

This chapter should be read in conjunction with Chapters 3–9, where the basic information which should be given to each ostomist has been discussed. It is with that background in mind that problems and their treatment have been outlined in this chapter and in Chapters 16 and 17. Many of the areas considered in this chapter will be interrelated. A careful history of *all* the problems must be taken from each patient, in order that a clear picture of what these problems are may result. It can then be established how best they may be dealt with. In almost all cases the size of the stoma, the site within which it is placed, and the type of effluent emerging from it will need to be considered, regardless of the problem with which the patient presents.

THE STOMA AND SURROUNDING SKIN

PROBLEMS WITH THE STOMA

Bleeding

Stomas are formed from a section of everted bowel tissue which is highly vascular and not normally exposed outside the body. Small amounts of blood are sometimes noticeable on the material used for cleaning the stoma and surrounding area. This is no more serious than the slight amount of bleeding which may occur when teeth are brushed vigorously, causing slight damage to the gums. Patients should be acquainted with this fact whilst being taught their own stoma care, so that they will not be alarmed if minimal bleeding occurs.

Soft white toilet paper, used either moist or dry, is an excellent material for cleaning the stoma and surrounding skin. It is gentle to use and easily flushed down the toilet for disposal.

Bleeding from the stoma may arise if tincture of benzoin is sprayed onto the stoma as well as the peristomal skin, when being used to enhance the adhesive properties of appliance plasters and to provide a good skin barrier. Care must be taken to avoid spraying the stoma with this substance.

Severe bleeding from the stoma can be due to a number of factors. Acute peptic ulceration may be produced by drugs such as aspirin, anticoagulants and some of the anti-inflammatory drugs used in arthritic conditions. Erosion of a blood vessel by the spread of malignancy may produce a sudden severe haemorrhage, which may present via the stoma or rectally if the patient has had a palliative defunctioning colostomy without removal of the tumour. Such a patient will show all the signs and symptoms of acute haemorrhage, and medical aid must be sought immediately.

Simulated bleeding may occur as a result of the taking of certain foodstuffs or drugs which discolour urine or faeces. Large quantities of blackcurrant juice or beetroot eaten in sufficient quantities may alter the colour of faeces for the bowel ostomist. Discolouration due to drugs is discussed in Chapter 13.

It must not be forgotten that iron medication with resultant black faeces may mask a severe melaena, and nurses must be alert in observing and reporting signs of the latter.

Prolapse

This is more commonly found in the transverse defunctioning colostomy, and may occur very occasionally in the ileostomy or ileal conduit. Prolapse can present with varying degrees of severity: extreme cases may have a prolapse of bowel 30–40cms (12–18 inches) in length, which is a horrifying spectacle for the patient, frequently directed to the hospital casualty department. If the patient is seen soon after the prolapse has occurred the experienced nurse or doctor may be able to reduce the stoma to its normal size using the following technique. The patient is placed supine, with one pillow, and encouraged to relax. A sedative may be ordered by the doctor if necessary. Wearing gloves, the nurse or doctor will attempt to reduce the prolapse by gently stroking the stoma in the direction of the aperture of the abdominal wall from whence it extrudes. In some instances the patient may be taught to repeat this procedure whilst the bag is in situ, so that it falls back into place.

A firm abdominal support which incorporates a St Mark's Hospital Plate may be ordered by the surgeon. This appliance is *never* used if the stoma is irreducible, as ulceration or gangrene, or both, may occur due to direct pressure on the bowel. Surgical intervention with refashioning of the stoma may be necessary.

Many elderly patients endure with fortitude a large prolapsed colostomy, if their surgeons deem further surgery inadvisable. Such patients need constant help and encouragement from both community and stoma care nurses, to ensure that their stomal equipment is adequate and manageable.

Retraction

This may be the result of the patient gaining weight, or because progression of a malignant tumour produces a fixed mass immediately in the vicinity of the stoma. The problems which arise vary with the different types of stomas, and will be considered separately.

Ileostomy retraction may also produce a narrowing at the neck of the stoma, which gives rise to intermittent obstructive episodes. Surgical intervention will relieve this, and the patient may need new equipment with a different size of opening following this surgery.

Colostomy retraction may also produce narrowing of the stoma neck. Digital examination of the stoma is carried out by the surgeon to see whether dilatation of the stoma is likely to be beneficial. The patient can be taught to use a St Mark's Hospital Dilator or a gloved finger where appropriate.

The patient should be advised not to become constipated, and a diet survey may prove of use to ensure that the patient's eating habits are conducive to producing a normal stool. The dietitian may suggest helpful additions to the patient's normal diet (see Chapter 12).

Surgical intervention may be necessary if the patient shows frequent signs of impacted faeces, a condition which manifests itself as spurious diarrhoea in the presence of large hard faeces blocking the stomal exit.

Ileal conduit retraction causes frequent leakage problems, since the urine is delivered at skin level via a distorted uneven exit. In some cases this is caused by the formation of alkaline crystals which cut into the stoma. The resultant scar tissue rapidly destroys a well-formed stoma, reducing it to a flattened misshapened blob, where it is difficult to see the aperture. The crystals are increased by being frequently bathed in a strongly alkaline urine, and an appliance with a non-return valve should be advised to prevent puddling of urine around the stoma. The use of equipment with a firm convex face-plate and a belt may help reduce leakage, as a firm, even pressure in the peristomal area encourages the stoma to stand proud. The surgeon may consider refashioning of the stoma where frequent leakage problems occur.

It has been found that vinegar neutralises the alkaline crystals, and the stoma may be dabbed with vinegar at each appliance change to aid this process. One ml of vinegar syringed into the appliance through the exit tap both morning and evening, after the appliance has been emptied, helps prevent the bag from becoming malodorous. Cleansing of the rubber non-disposable bags is also improved by the use of vinegar: antiseptic solutions tend to leave a slimy deposit on the inner surface.

Colour of the stoma
The stoma should be a healthy pink, and any deviation from this colour should be noted and reported to the doctor. Immediately post-operatively a dark purple stoma indicates a poor blood supply, and medical advice should be sought promptly. The condition can improve gradually as the patient's general condition improves, but careful frequent observation must be carried out. If the surgeon ascribes discolouration to lack of blood supply he may decide to operate to remove a pre-gangrenous section of bowel.

Occasionally the condition *melanosis coli* is found at surgery. This is a dark brown or black discolouration of the colon, caused by the patient taking frequent strong purgatives. This condition must be recorded by both the hospital and family practitioner in the patient's medical notes, to prevent the stoma colour being thought to be due to a poor blood supply at a later date.

A pale colourless stoma indicates a severe anaemia; other signs of this condition are normally also apparent.

Ulceration of the stoma
This may be caused by an ill-fitting appliance: too small an aperture will either cut or ulcerate the stoma. It occurs mainly when a prolapse or enlargement of the stoma is present, and a change to a suitably styled bag with correct aperture allows the ulceration to heal.

Ulceration may also be caused by an appliance which depends only on a belt to maintain its position, and which has no adhesive to secure it. If the stoma site is unsuitable for such a bag, the flange see-saws around the stoma as the patient moves, producing ulceration. Change to a more suitable appliance improves the condition rapidly.

Severing of the stoma
This can occasionally occur when vigorous exercise is undertaken while wearing a sliding appliance as described above, or as the result of road traffic accidents. Some authorities suggest that ostomists should not wear seat belts, but discussion has not brought a definite answer to this

question. The severed stoma should be covered with a firm petroleum jelly dressing, and medical aid sought promptly. Refashioning of the stoma may be necessary.

Papillomata of the stoma

These may occur singly or in large numbers, causing an altered surface of the stoma. No surgical intervention is usually required, unless the surgeon decides a biopsy is advisable.

Stenosis of urinary stomas

This may be a long term consequence of inadequate blood supply to the conduit. There is progressive fibrosis and constriction of the outlet leading to pooling of the urine in the conduit, with urinary reabsorption, infection and dilation of the upper urinary tract. Dilation of the stoma with a catheter or small finger may be all the treatment that is required, but usually surgical intervention is necessary.

Epithelialisation of the stoma tends to occur over a long period of time and may contribute to stoma stenosis. Squamous epithelium grows in from the surrounding skin to replace the bowel mucosa, and this gives the stoma a pearly-white corrugated appearance. The caustic agent silver nitrate may be used with care to remove this excess tissue.

PROBLEMS WITH THE SKIN SURROUNDING THE STOMA

Skin problems tend to fall into three main categories: those which are caused by a reaction of the patient to the bag adhesive or skin protective agent; those which are caused by an appliance which is unsuitable for the patient's current needs; and those due to other causes. Skin problems caused by inappropriate use of appliances are discussed in this chapter (see page 192). It must be remembered that many patients do not come for advice until their skin is actually sore or causes them pain. Marked redness and even a broken skin may not appear to them to be a problem, and ostomists need encouragement to seek advice at an early stage, before the problems multiply and are less easy to resolve.

Skin reactions

Some patients' skin reacts strongly to the adhesive plaster of their appliance. Recurrent application of the bag results in perpetual skin problems around the stoma. It can also result in widespread manifestation, with severe skin irritation and a rash involving the whole body surface. The patient rapidly becomes demoralised. Treatment includes establishing which type of adhesive plasters cause skin problems for the individual patient. Patch tests with a number of different types of adhesive and skin protective aids may be useful for patients who develop sensitivity to most plasters. With this information the patient can choose one of the following solutions:

1) To continue with his usual appliance, but to use a skin protective aid to prevent the adhesive coming in contact with his skin;
2) To change to an appliance with an adhesive suitable for his skin;
3) To minimise removal of bags from his skin by using a two-piece appliance. A skin protective aid can be used in addition to the two-piece appliance, or as an integral part of the appliance flange.

Skin barriers include the special adhesive sprays and non-oily creams marketed for stoma care, karaya and Stomahesive; reactions to these occur occasionally. The cure is the removal of the cause, and a new skin barrier must be found to which the patient does not react. Stomahesive rarely produces skin problems: a slight pinkish colour of the skin in very fair patients may occur, but this is acceptable. The very small number of patients who have severe reactions to karaya should be advised to use an appliance without a washer of this material.

Other causes of skin problems

Hirsute patients may develop folliculitis as a result of either shaving, or pulling out hairs when the appliance is removed. An adhesive remover such as Dow Corning Medical Adhesive Remover may be helpful in removing the appliance without trauma. Epilation may be considered pre-operatively to ensure a hair-free area at the stoma site, and electrolysis used to achieve this. Exacerbation of other skin problems, such as psoriasis, may cause a flare-up of skin problems in the stomal area. This usually settles once treatment of the overall condition becomes effective.

Bacterial and fungal infections may infrequently be found in the peristomal area. Swabs should be sent to the Bacteriology Department to establish the type of organism and its sensitivity to antibacterial or antifungal agents. The method of treatment should be suitable for use with appliances: oily creams or ointments can cause problems with adherence of the appliance, and are therefore rarely satisfactory.

Common methods of treating proven skin infections include the following:

1) Use of an antibiotic or antifungal spray to which the organism is sensitive;

2) Use of an antifungal powder followed by Opsite spray, to provide a surface to which the appliance will adhere;
3) Use of a combined anti-inflammatory and appropriate antibacterial or antifungal spray where severe skin damage has occurred.

Further swabs should be sent to the Bacteriology Department on completion of any of these courses of treatment, to check whether the infection has been eradicated.

A hairdryer is sometimes helpful for drying off the skin, either before or after application of the spray. A small cap from a bottle or jar may be filled with gauze and held over the stoma during this procedure, to prevent soiling of the skin if the stoma is active.

Routine use of antibacterial agents for skin protection is not normally advisable. It is not yet known whether such agents are absorbed through the mucosal surface of the stoma and, if so, what effect on the body this would have over an extensive period. The emergence of resistant organisms, after prolonged use of antibiotics to combat infection in other areas, would also indicate that routine topical use in stoma care is probably unwise. Further research in these areas is required.

APPLIANCES AND THEIR USE

PROBLEMS WITH BAGS

Few appliances prove faulty, because of the very strict quality control and rigorous tests to which manufacturing companies subject them. Patients should be advised that where two or three appliances in a batch are found to be faulty the *used* bags, washed clean of effluent, should be returned to the manufacturer (not the chemist), with the batch slip or code number where possible, and details of the fault found. It may be helpful if one or two unused appliances from the same batch are also returned for investigation by the manufacturer.

Emptying devices on the urinary bags should be tested by the patient before he leaves the house. Clamps on ileostomy and drainable colostomy bags should be strong, secure, simple in design and manageable by the patient. These features are of special importance for those handicapped with poor vision and arthritic hands. A large bag clamp may cause great discomfort if the stoma is badly sited and the emptying spout of the appliance lies across the groin fold.

STYLES OF APPLIANCES

The type of equipment must be suitable for the stoma.

Urinary diversion
The bag must have a tap for emptying, and have a suitable connection for use with a night drainage tube and bag. The volume of urine excreted during sleep is greater than the capacity of urostomy bags, and can cause severe leakage problems at night if not drained off. A bag which has a non-return valve is superior to those without, as this prevents puddling of urine in the vicinity of the stoma with the resultant undermining of the adhesive.

Night drainage equipment for the urostomist
During the hours of sleep the urostomy bag will usually be attached to a tube, allowing drainage of urine into a large bag, and thus preventing overflow and leakage. The night drainage bag should be attached to a wire frame or hanger, which may be attached to the bed or be free standing (see Figure 15.1). Whilst the night drainage bag is in situ the tubing must be checked for kinks and dips which would prevent the urine flowing freely into the bag. Particular care must be taken to make sure the section where the tubing connects with the night bag is straight (see Figure 15.2). The commonest cause of leakage at night from a urostomy bag is night drainage equipment that has been incorrectly set up, preventing urine from draining into it, with the resultant overflow from the urostomy bag leaking into the bed.

Problems with night drainage at home can be avoided if the patient is taught how to set up his equipment correctly, and uses a suitable hanger for his bag, consistent with the height and style of his bed.

Patients who do not wish to connect up to a night drainage bag may find a leg bag less restricting, particularly if they change position frequently. Others prefer to wake once or twice during the night to empty their urostomy bags, and may need to use alarm clocks, at least initially, to establish a pattern of waking at suitable intervals. Curtailment of fluid intake during the evening, so that urinary output is reduced at night, is inadvisable. An output of 1000–1800ml per 24 hours is thought to reduce the risk of urinary infection or stone formation, and patients should be advised to have a good fluid intake spread over their normal hours of waking.

The illustrations on the following pages indicate three aspects of stoma siting and its management.

Figures 1 and 2 are examples of how good siting can be achieved through pre-operative assessment of the patient's abdomen.

Figures 3, 6 and 7 indicate problems which may arise when stoma sites are not determined pre-operatively.

Figures 4, 5 and 8 show that traditional stoma sites may not necessarily be the most appropriate ones for individual patients. Reference should be made to the operation notes, to establish the type of stoma which has been formed and the type of effluent which should therefore be expected from it.

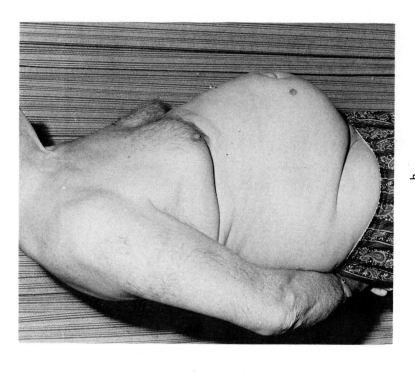

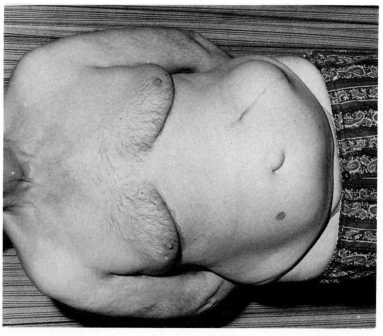

b

a

Figure 1   Good siting of a stoma on an obese patient, avoiding bones, bulges and the umbilicus.
a) Front view, standing. b) Side view, standing.

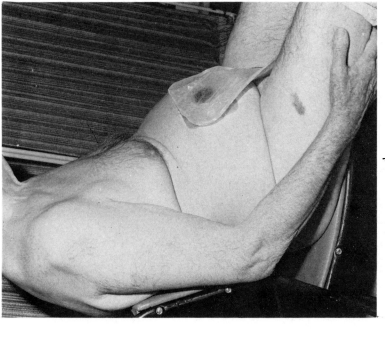

c

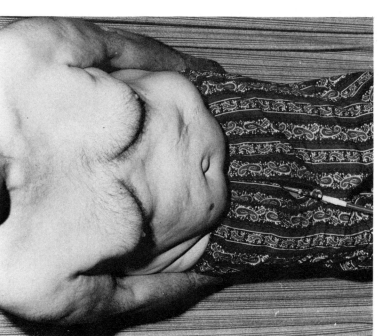

d

Figure 1 Good siting of a stoma on an obese patient, avoiding bones, bulges and the umbilicus. c) The patient is standing but leaning forward, demonstrating a change in abdominal contour. d) Patient sitting with the appliance in situ.

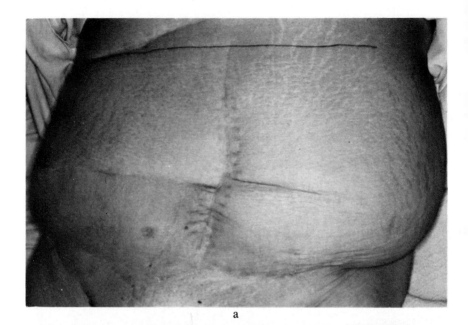

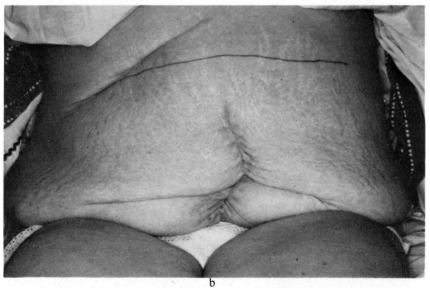

Figure 2 Siting a stoma for a patient with a flabby abdomen and scars from previous surgery. a) Patient lying flat in bed. The normal waistline is marked. b) Patient sitting up in bed, front view. Compare Figures b) and c) where there appears to be quite a spacious abdomen on which to site the stoma, with the fore-shortened view which is presented when the patient sits in a chair instead of in bed in Figure e)

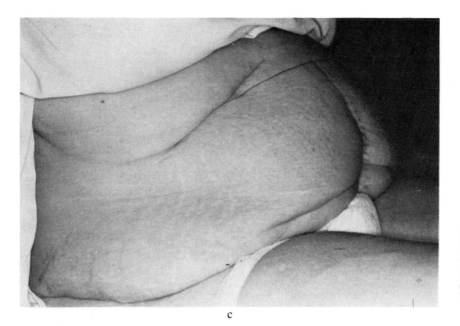

c

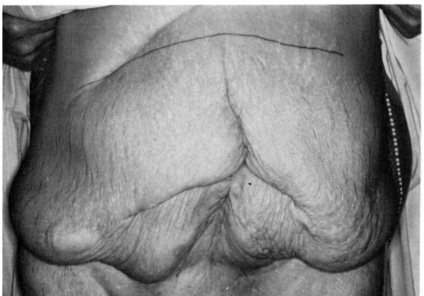

d

Figure 2 Siting a stoma for a patient with a flabby abdomen and scars from previous surgery. c) Patient sitting up in bed, showing right side of abdomen. d) Patient standing. Note the pendulous abdominal folds shown here in comparison to Figure a).

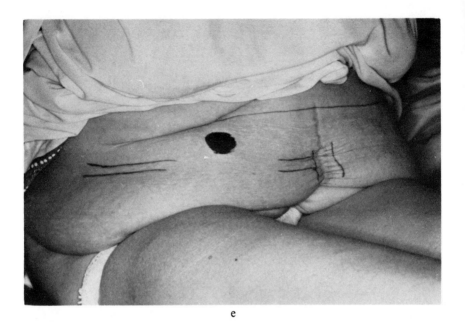

e

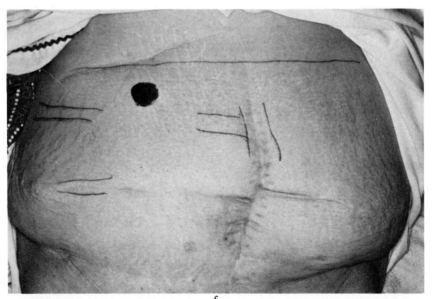

f

Figure 2 Siting a stoma for a patient with a flabby abdomen and scars from previous surgery. e) Patient sitting in a chair. Note the site for an ileal conduit is well clear of the waistline, abdominal creases and scar. f) Patient lying flat in bed. Compare this deceptively flat view of the abdomen with Figures d) and e).

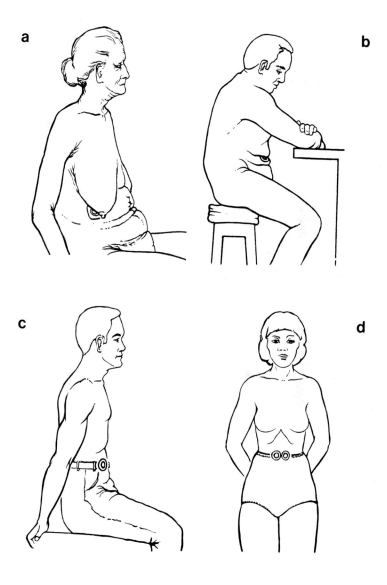

Figure 3 Examples of awkward siting of stomas. a) Female patient with stoma obscured by large pendulous breast. b) Stoma sunk in fatty folds. c) Male patient with stoma on waistline under waistband of trousers. d) Female patient with waistline stoma constricted by waistband of underclothes.

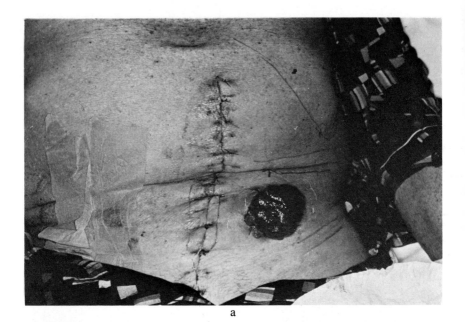

a

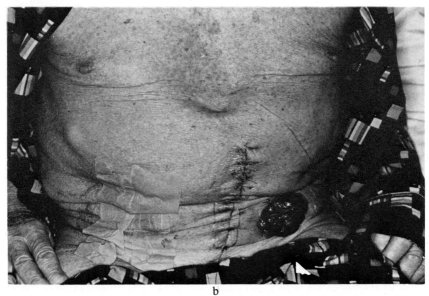

b

Figure 4 Transverse colostomy sited pre-operatively on the patient's left side. There was no suitable area on the right side, where a transverse colostomy would normally be positioned. a) Patient in bed, lying back against the pillows. b) Patient sitting up, demonstrating creases on the right side of the abdomen and an enlarged rib cage on both sides leaving little room for a stoma.

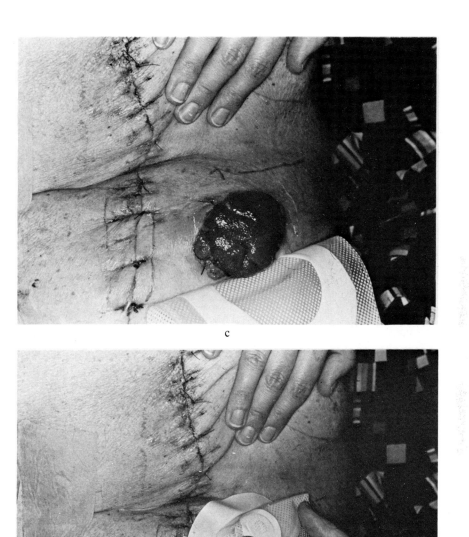

c

d

Figure 4   c) Fold of skin above the stoma pulled up to create a flat surface immediately around the stoma. d) Pliable flanged bag moulding easily into place.

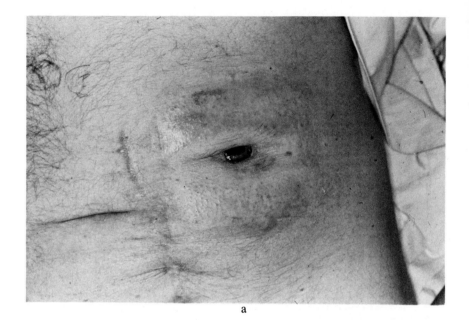

a

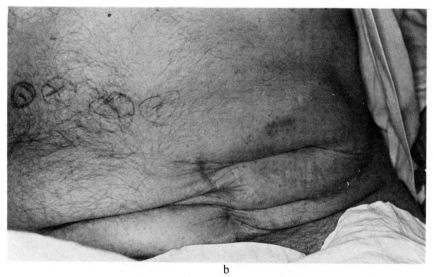

b

Figure 5   This patient was found at operation to have limited suitable bowel from which to fashion his urinary stoma. The flush urinary stoma was therefore sited on the left during the operation, and not on the usual right side of the abdomen. He is now being marked for a transverse colostomy. a) Patient lying in bed. Flush urinary stoma visible. b) Patient sitting up. Note disappearance of urinary stoma into a fold of flesh on the left. Deep creases on the right of the body make it necessary to site the transverse colostomy high up.

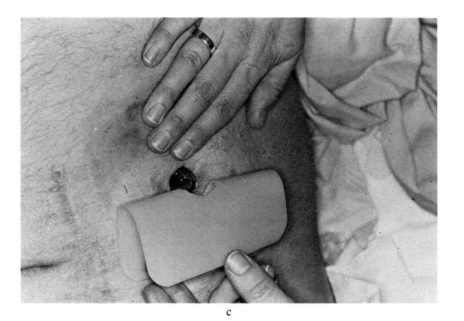

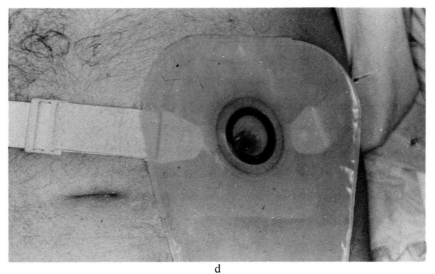

Figure 5   c) Stomahesive is applied, with the overhanging fold of skin pulled up, creating a flat surface. d) Appliance and belt well in place. Note that the sites marked as suitable for the transverse colostomy are well clear of the urostomy belt.

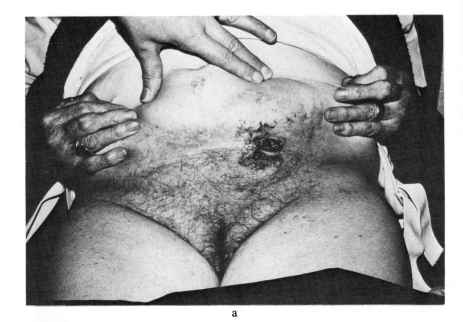

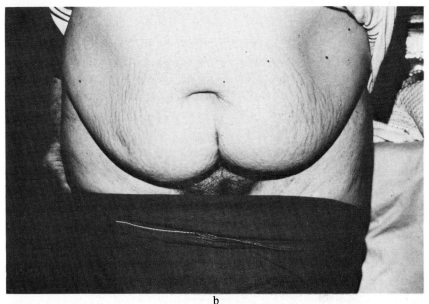

Figure 6   Stoma raised without pre-operative siting. The position of the stoma was decided upon when the patient was in theatre, in the Trendelenburg and semilithotomy position. a) Patient lying flat. Stoma sited much too low. b) Patient standing. The stoma is hidden by an apron of fat, making application of a bag extremely difficult.

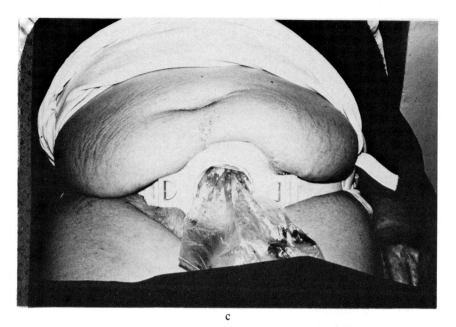

c

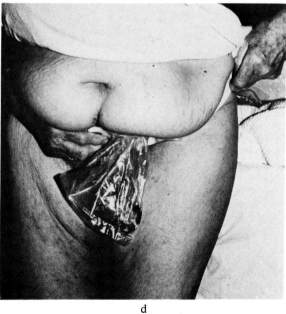

d

Figure 6   c) Patient fitted with an appliance with a rigid flange and belt to push up the apron of fat. d) Patient standing, appliance in situ.

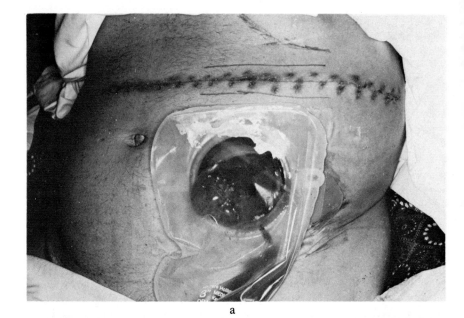

a

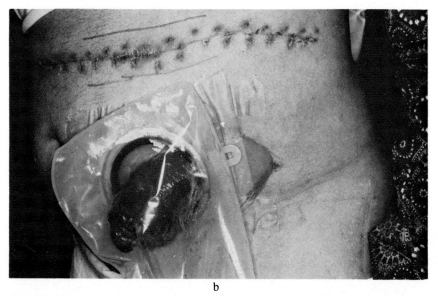

b

Figure 7 This patient was unexpectedly found to require a transverse colostomy while undergoing other surgery, and the stoma site therefore had to be decided upon during the operation. a) The patient is lying in bed. The stoma is well clear of his umbilicus and scar, but rather close to the groin crease. b) Patient standing, producing a fairly crease-free abdomen for application of his bag. However, the position of the stoma is now too low for the patient to see where to apply his bag.

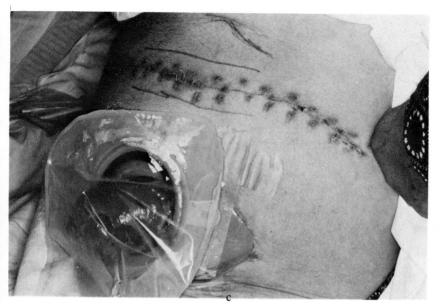

Figure 7   c) The patient is sitting. Note the more pronounced groin crease than in a), and that the appliance flange is now resting on top of his thigh. The appliance plaster is unlikely to adhere well to the wrinkled skin in the groin, making containment of the semi-fluid faeces difficult.

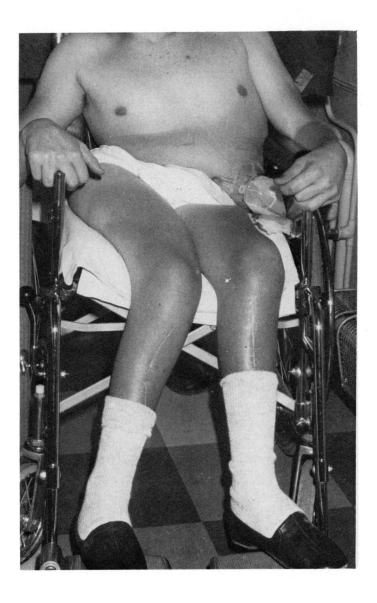

Figure 8   Patient in a wheelchair. The urinary stoma is sited on the left where there is a larger area of flat abdomen than in the more usual right-sided position.

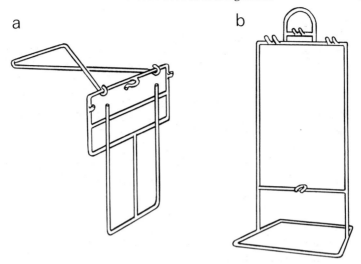

Figure 15.1   Night drainage hangers. a) For attachment to the bed.
b) Free standing.

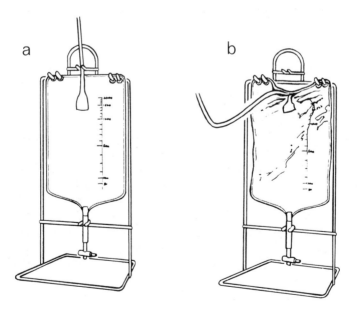

Figure 15.2   a) Night drainage bag correctly positioned on stand.
b) *Incorrectly* positioned bag, with a kink in the section of tubing where
it joins the night drainage bag.

Ileostomy
The effluent from this type of stoma is never formed, but a toothpaste-like consistency may be achieved. A drainable appliance is required, which can be emptied several times a day when necessary.

Right-sided or transverse colostomy
Patients with this type of colostomy may need a drainable appliance, because of a semi-solid or fluid stool. The addition of bran and high fibre bulking agents to the diet frequently produces a firmer, less frequent stool, which may be manageable by means of a non-drainable bag. The individual patient's preference and facilities at home and at work influence the choice.

Left sigmoid colostomy
A formed stool of normal consistency is passed by many patients with this type of stoma. Regular eating habits can produce a regular evacuation in some patients. Most patients prefer a non-drainable bag, which can be changed two or three times daily, but too frequent changes can cause skin irritation. This may be overcome by the use of two-piece appliances, skin barrier creams and hypo-allergenic types of adhesive.

APPLIANCE APERTURE AND STOMA SHRINKAGE

All the above stomas usually shrink quite noticeably during the first two weeks after surgery, and the stoma must be measured to ensure the correct size aperture is being used, i.e. 3mm (⅛ inch) larger than the stoma. The stoma should be measured again after six weeks and six months, as by then the optimum size is usually reached. Excoriation presenting as a small angry area surrounding the stoma is frequently due to use of equipment with too large an aperture, leaving the skin exposed to contact with the effluent. This is particularly noticeable in the patient with an ileostomy, or an ascending or transverse colostomy, where the effluent will be more fluid and destructive of the skin.

Treatment consists of selection and application of suitable equipment. The stoma must be measured, and a drainable appliance with an aperture 3mm (⅛ inch) larger than the stoma selected. A skin barrier should be worn, such as Stomahesive. To ensure a leak-free situation, the hole is cut in the Stomahesive wafer to fit snugly around the stoma and the backing paper is then removed. Karaya paste may be squeezed onto the under-surface of the Stomahesive around the opening, and allowed to set for a few minutes. The wafer may then be placed in position, with the karaya forming a good seal beneath it, around the base of the stoma. The bag is then applied on top of the Stomahesive. As a further aid to skin protection, a tube of paper may be inserted through the opening of the drainable bag, and used as a funnel through which karaya powder may be puffed onto the immediate peristomal area. The karaya powder may coat the stoma during this process; this is not harmful. A marked improvement in the skin condition will normally be seen when the appliance is changed two or three days following this method of skin care. Holes caused by skin-edge separation adjacent to the stoma may also be treated in this way.

Use of too large an aperture in a urinary appliance man result in *pseudoepitheliamatous hyperplasia* or 'dish pan hands'. Skin constantly bathed in urine will become sodden and wrinkled, and in extreme cases may require surgical correction in the form of resiting the stoma, as it prevents the fitting of a leak proof appliance due to the distorted uneven skin surface. If the condition is treated early enough, it quickly resolves. Treatment consists of use of the correct size aperture in an appliance with a non-return valve, to prevent puddling of urine around the stoma.

LEAKAGE PROBLEMS

Patients may present with a problem of sore skin, which in fact is due to leakage. A careful history must be taken from patients who have leakage problems to establish whether there is a pattern in how, when or where the leaks occur. Change in weight may produce many of the situations discussed below. Evaluation of the current situation should be made so that suitable equipment may be advised.

A history of an appliance leaking consistently whenever a colostomist has loose stools may indicate that an appliance suitable for formed faeces only is being worn. Elimination of the loose stools through the use of bran, a suitable diet or medication (see Chapters 12 and 13) will remove the cause of the leaks, and the patient can continue wearing his usual bag.

A history of consistent leaks from one or two points of the bag – particularly at the sides – indicates the likely presence of a gulley caused by skin folds, scars and puckering of the abdominal surface, along which the effluent tracks. The patient should be seen without an appliance, standing, sitting and lying down, and in any other typical position where leaks occur, e.g. in the bucket car seat position. This procedure almost always reveals the offending gulleys, and also allows the stoma site to be assessed in relation to the ribs and pelvic bones, umbilicus and abdominal scars (see siting section between pages 190 and 191). Treatment consists of filling in the gulleys to even out the abdominal surface. An application of karaya paste spread into the gulleys with a throat spatula, and allowed to dry, will create an even surface. The paste may then be sprayed with Dow Corning Medical Adhesive, to produce a tacky consistency, and the bag of choice placed in position. Such patients almost invariably need to wear an appliance with a belt, to provide firm pressure to maintain the equipment in position. Alternatively, pieces of Stomahesive may be used to fill in the gulleys, with a square of Stomahesive placed on top so that the abdominal surface is even before a suitable bag is applied.

Weight gain may produce an overhang of flesh above the stoma, which may be readily observed when the patient stands up. The result may be direction of the stoma effluent downwards onto the skin immediately below the stoma, which becomes red and sore, and leakage below the stoma occurs. For many patients this problem can be easily resolved by use of an appliance with a firm flange and a belt, to curb the overhang and allow the stoma to direct its effluent outwards into the bag. Some patients need to build up the area beneath the stoma, to bring it level with the overhang, and a half square of Stomahesive or half a karaya washer is suitable for this purpose. A bag with a semi-rigid flange may then be applied as above.

Leakage problems caused by bones which are too close to the stoma are not uncommon. Appliances with a semi-rigid flange are not suitable, because the flange will see-saw every time the hip or lower rib margin comes in contact with it. The appliance of choice will be a flat, flexible bag which can mould around both the stoma and the adjacent bone.

Herniae may be peri-stomal, wound incisional, or the abdominal wall may be devoid of effective musculature, producing a flaccid apron of fat. An abdominal support will be required, but the type chosen must not impede the emptying of a drainable or urostomy bag. An opening in the support may be necessary to facilitate this. The colostomy patient wearing a non-drainable bag usually finds he can cope with a support which does not have an opening for the bag to protrude from. He will change his bag in the morning before putting on his support, and in the evening after removing it. Patients who wear supports to correct orthopaedic problems must be given extra consideration, to ensure that their stomal appliances are not dislodged by their special equipment.

CHANGES IN STOMAL ACTION

CONSTIPATION

This is rarely a problem for the patient with an ileostomy, or an ascending or transverse colostomy. The patient with a defunctioning colostomy may have effluent crossing the spur and becoming impacted in the distal loop. Treatment to resolve this situation must be given with care, particularly where the rectal growth has not been removed. Olive oil given via a Foley catheter into the distal loop of the stoma and per rectum twice daily for 48 hours will lubricate the bowel. A washout of warm water via the distal loop opening of the stoma may then be given to remove the faecal material (see Chapter 11).

The patient with a sigmoid colostomy may become constipated as a result of poor eating habits, and advice should be given on establishing a more suitable diet (see Chapter 12).

The ostomist who requires regular analgesics will be likely to become constipated, because of the slowing down of gut activity which many analgesics produce (see Chapter 13). Such a patient must be informed of this side effect of his pain-relieving drugs, and advised to take a regular aperient such as Dorbanex or Duphalac. It is important that the patient with chronic pain is encouraged to take both analgesics and aperients regularly, rather than to reduce his analgesics and suffer pain, in an attempt to avoid constipation.

Instillation of olive oil or a warm water enema may be necessary to remove constipated faeces. Both are best given via a Foley catheter, with the balloon blown up to 10–15ml to prevent immediate leakage back through the sphincterless stoma. The catheter should not be left in situ for more than ten minutes.

Constipation with overflow, or spurious diarrhoea, is the escape of faecal fluid in the presence of impacted faeces. This may present either as diarrhoea or constipation, but a history of alternating fluid and rock-like faeces being passed is indicative of this condition, and digital examination of the stoma usually reveals the impaction.

Treatment consists of removing the faeces as described above. Aperients may also be necessary to clear impacted faeces lodged higher up the bowel. A careful explanation of the rationale of such treatment must be given to the patient, particularly if he presents with the problem of diarrhoea, or he is unlikely to follow the treatment through and may seek drugs to constipate him, thus prolonging his problem. Dietary advice may be required if the patient's eating habits are such that the problem is likely to recur.

DIARRHOEA

In the ileostomist a copious fluid effluent resembling cold milkless tea which contains shreds of mucus is very suggestive of a mechanical obstruction. The patient rapidly becomes dehydrated and develops electrolyte imbalance, and prompt medical treatment is essential. Surgery may be necessary to remove or free the adhesions.

In the colostomist a loose stool may be caused by incorrect diet, drugs, or further disease of the bowel such as cancer, diverticulitis or Crohn's disease. Where it is suspected that diarrhoea is caused by recurrence of disease, medical attention should be sought promptly. Drug-induced diarrhoea may be intentional or unintentional. *Intentionally induced diarrhoea* prior to closure of a colostomy may be achieved by sufficient Mist Magnesium Sulphate being given to clear the proximal colon, with the necessary oral fluids to prevent dehydration. *Unintentionally induced diarrhoea* may be produced by a number of drugs including antibiotics, anti-tumour drugs, and medication given in preparation for some X-rays (see Chapter 13).

Treatment consists of establishing the cause and treating it. A suitable drainable bag should be suggested to help contain the effluent and prevent frequent bag changes; and advice given on diet and medication to help alleviate the diarrhoea. This has been discussed in Chapters 12, 13 and 14.

Colostomists who travel abroad should be advised to take a small supply of drainable bags with them, as a complete change in diet occasionally produces diarrhoea. Advice on drugs for the treatment of diarrhoea should be sought by both ileostomists and colostomists before travel, and suitable medication may be prescribed by the doctor to take if required.

QUESTIONS FOR DISCUSSION

1) How may minimal bleeding of the stoma be explained to the patient in a way which will not alarm him?

2) How may a stoma which is prolapsed be dealt with in the early stages?

3) What complications may retraction of the stoma present in the following cases: a) ileostomy; b) colostomy; c) ileal conduit?

4) Which type of appliance is suitable for the following: a) urinary diversion; b) ileostomy; c) transverse colostomy; d) left sigmoid colostomy?

5) What may occur as a result of a patient with a left sigmoid colostomy being prescribed regular analgesics? How may this condition be treated?

6) In the case of an ileostomist, what would a copious effluent resembling cold milkless tea containing shreds of mucus indicate?

7) What addition to the diet may help to produce a less fluid and less frequent stool in the patient with a colostomy?

8) What advice would you give to a beer-drinker who has a colostomy?

Chapter 16

Lifestyle Problems of the Ostomist and his Family

RESUMPTION OF NORMAL LIFESTYLE

The average ostomist worries about potential problems, even when provided with all the information available today, and no effort should be spared to build up the patient's confidence before his discharge from hospital. Nurses can do much to show the patient that he is acceptable socially, by encouraging him to participate in ward activities such as visiting the lounge to watch television, attending hospital church services, and eating at the ward communal dining table.

Belief that the ostomist can wear his normal clothing can be fostered by encouraging him to have his own clothes brought into hospital, so that he can get dressed. Short walks or an afternoon out with friends or family can do much to convince the ostomist that nobody in the outside world perceives him as different, and that his appliance is not discernable.

Most new ostomists worry about staying away from home, and advice and encouragement to take the plunge should be given as outlined in Chapter 7. The nurse can help remove the anxieties of patient and family by encouraging them to discuss holiday plans. A trial run of a weekend visiting friends may be of value in helping him decide what type of accommodation and facilities he would like to book for his holiday.

Family and friends can also be guided by the nurse in ways to ensure the ostomist does not curtail social activities where he may be offered food and drink. Their encouragement and support on the ostomist's first meal out in a restaurant, or first visit to his local pub, can do much to help him back to these normal activities. By making sure the ostomist is eating a full and varied diet before he leaves hospital the nurse sets the stage for this to continue after discharge. Advice on food and drink has been outlined in Chapter 12. Beer drinkers may be advised to take extra bran before imbibing their normal quota of pints.

Returning to work should be discussed before the patient leaves hospital, even though this may lie some months ahead (see Chapter 7). The patient who is encouraged to discuss potential problems with his doctors and nurses will return to work confident that if problems do arise there are people to whom he can turn, and who have the authority to give him informed support. Where extensive surgery has made return to a heavy manual job inadvisable, a combined approach by the ostomist, employer, Disablement Resettlement Officer and union representative (if he is a union member) can result in suitable employment or retraining being made available.

Problems occasionally arise when the ostomist returns to work if his employer has a misconception of the nature of stoma surgery, particularly in the food industry if the ostomist is incorrectly viewed as a health hazard. It must be stressed that ostomists who worked in food industries prior to surgery remain suitable for such work after surgery. Informal discussion between the stoma care nurse and the employer usually results in a more informed approach by the latter. A letter from the surgeon to the employer's medical officer, outlining the surgery performed and his medical assessment as fit to return to work can be most useful.

Where problems over disposal of bags at work arise, the occupational health nurse may be able to arrange facilities for disposal in the works departmental surgery.

ATTITUDES TOWARDS DISEASE AND STOMA SURGERY

The patient who has a long term history of ulcerative colitis or Crohn's disease will have endured pain, indignity and humiliation. His frequent visits to the toilet, malodorous effluent, occasional soiling of clothing, and attacks of debilitating illness will encourage him to seek surgery for a release from the anguish associated with his disease. This will be sought more strongly if he has talked to someone who has shed such a miserable existence by undergoing panproctocolectomy. Most of these patients have extensive knowledge of their disease, having consulted medical text books and dictionaries, but still have many questions they need to ask. Trust in the hospital staff must be built up through time spent on informed explanations, so that such patients feel they can return for help at any time in the future. Given this support, most patients with ulcerative colitis accept their surgery; belief that it is curative helps enormously.

The patient who has an ileostomy as treatment for acute fulminating colitis cannot believe that after such a short illness he is in need of such radical surgery. Unlimited time and patience must be spent to help him believe that this surgery was the right decision.

Patients with Crohn's disease may suffer episodes of abdominal pain as a result of recurrence even after stoma surgery, because this disease can affect any part of the gastrointestinal tract. At such times these patients can appear resentful that in spite of extensive surgery they are not cured. Extra understanding of their problems in accepting both disease and a stoma must be shown by nursing and medical staff.

Patients who have had cancer of either the bowel or bladder, which has been removed by surgery, will usually come to terms with their stoma and the knowledge that they have had a malignant condition. It takes time for such patients to be convinced they have benefited by surgery; every ache or unexplained pain may be seen as heralding a recurrence in the early months after surgery. The patient's visits to the out-patient department should not be taken lightly by staff; they are his lifeline, and he feels safe when he is told that his next appointment will be in six month's time. Coupled with this must be a system engendering easy access to the stoma clinic, so that problems can be dealt with promptly, and fears of a return of the cancer dispelled appropriately.

Some patients with cancer have palliative stoma surgery. It is a hard burden for both patient and family to know that he has both a stoma and his disease, and acceptance is difficult, particularly if the stoma, while diverting faecal or urinary effluent, does not relieve vaginal or rectal discharge, or relieve pain.

Support for the patient and his family to come to terms with such a situation must be given through a combined effort by all health care workers in hospital and community. This may be aided by others such as friends, neighbours, and ministers of religion.

PERSONAL RELATIONSHIPS

There are many questions asked by the patient about to undergo stoma surgery, and time must be given for each patient to ask what he wants to know in his own way. As one young man put it 'What about the old sex thing, Sis? Please do not think I am promiscuous, I am just normal.' Other questions asked regularly include:

– Will I be smelly and objectionable to others?
– Can people tell by looking at me that I am different?
– Will I need to sleep in a different room from my marriage partner?
– Do I have to sleep in a separate bed?
– Will I be able to marry and have a family?

Most of these questions can be answered with truthful reassurance, as modern improved stomal equipment is odourproof, undetectable and most reliable. Married partners do not need to sleep separately; this is a time when a loving shoulder to nestle against is needed more than ever before.

Many ostomists do not wish to discuss their surgery with any but their nearest and dearest, and the joining of a society is abhorrent to them. Their wishes must be respected, and no-one should be pressed to become a member of a voluntary association. On the other hand, many people gain a great deal of confidence from seeing others who have returned to a normal lifestyle after similar operations. Each patient should be treated in the very individual manner that their personality requires.

SEXUAL ATTRACTIVENESS AND ABILITY

Sexual attractiveness and ability have been discussed in Chapters 1, 5, 6 and 7. Many of the fears of the ostomist about his or her attractiveness may be minimised by the partner watching how to change an appliance before the ostomist leaves hospital, and thus seeing the exposed stoma. This decision must always be made by the couple concerned, as what will be helpful for some couples is not for others.

Low pelvic surgery in the *male* may result in impaired sexual ability. This may only occur temporarily, if at all, in the ileostomist whose surgeon employs an intersphincteric approach to remove the rectum. The male undergoing radical cystectomy for removal of bladder cancer will have a more widespread excision, and damage of the nerves frequently results in impotence. A number of men undergoing removal of rectal cancer also become impotent following damage of the *nervi erigentes*. In selected cases only, silicone penile implants may be resorted to, to enable the man to achieve an erection.

Female patients may experience discomfort when love-making is first resumed after operation. The adoption of different positions often eliminates the discomfort, and pleasurable experiences are regained. Scarring following removal of the bladder or rectum may make intercourse painful for some women. Their partners should be advised that if the woman has had her bladder removed it may be more comfortable if the man is on top (i.e. his penis points towards the posterior vaginal wall and away from the scarring). But if the rectum has been removed the woman may find it more comfortable to be uppermost, when the penis will then point towards the anterior vaginal wall. Lack of lubrication may be a problem, and some authorities advocate the use of K–Y jelly to aid easy penetration.

The reader has been bombarded with a host of problems which ostomists may have, and suggestions of how they may best be dealt with. It must be said that the improvement in surgical techniques, medical care and specialised nursing care, and the wealth of improved equipment now available, have decreased the number of problems once suffered by most ostomists. Difficulties now encountered by patients should be speedily and efficiently solved. The days of the tormenting problems some patients were expected to endure are over.

Chapter 17

Sources of Help for Nurses
and Ostomists

Information and advice on most aspects of stoma care is increasingly becoming available through all members of the health care team. *Hospital and family doctors* join with *hospital and community nurses* to provide a generalised service, and liaise with the *stoma care nurse* who can provide specialised information and expertise, as discussed in Chapter 18.

Most stoma care nurses, and an increasing number of other nurses with ostomy patients, are joining *The Royal College of Nursing (Rcn) Stoma Care Nursing Forum.* This was set up in 1977 to provide a national entity for nurses wanting to share knowledge and to exchange views on stoma care, as well as to run conferences with speakers discussing a wide variety of aspects of stoma care and current trends. Liaison has been established between the Forum and the DHSS, statutory and voluntary bodies concerned with stoma care, and the companies manufacturing or supplying stomal equipment.

Medical Social Workers help to ensure that the patient is not suffering financial distress because of his surgery or illness and that, where applicable, social security benefits may be obtained. Poor housing is investigated, and help sought from the local authority if rehousing is a necessity. Information is also available through the medical social workers of services such as Meals on Wheels, and of diseases where industrial compensation may be applied for, such as some cases of bladder cancer.

Disablement Resettlement Officers can give advice and help when a change of job or retraining is required following stoma surgery. Few ostomists are grossly disabled, but it is sometimes advantageous for an ostomist to be registered as disabled and so eligible for employment with a firm obliged to employ a quota of disabled people. This may result in more security in a job, with unavoidable sickness being viewed more leniently by the employer. The whereabouts of the nearest Disablement Resettlement Officer can be obtained from the local Social Security Office.

The Employment Medical Adviser is available to visit an ostomist's place of work. He can be requested by either the ostomist or his employer to give an informed opinion on the type of work suitable for the ostomist, and whether he can continue in the post held prior to surgery. Queries tend to arise in work connected with food or where lifting of heavy objects is required, and liaison between the surgeon and medical adviser may be helpful in considering individual cases. The Employment Medical Advisory Service is located at local offices of the Department of Employment.

Pharmacists both in hospital and the community obtain the stomal equipment the ostomist needs, and will encourage the patient to seek advice on medication or appliances when queries arise.

Sexual and Personal Relationships of the Disabled (SPOD) is an association which offers information and advice on sexual and related topics in an informed and sensitive manner, through personal discussion and reading material.

The Ileostomy Association of Great Britain and Ireland was formed in 1958 when ostomists were not satisfied with the after-care that was available. Self-help groups were formed, meetings held, and pressure for change applied in areas where improvements were needed. Meetings of branches of the IA are now held in many large towns and cities. Appliance firms attend the meetings to demonstrate new products, and talks are given by various speakers on topics of interest to ileostomists. The Ileostomy Association has many voluntary visitors who are willing to visit patients before and after surgery both in hospital and after discharge, to give encouragement by demonstrating their own return to a full and normal life. A quarterly IA Journal is issued to all members.

The *Colostomy Welfare Group* provides a similar visiting service to that of the Ileostomy Association. Meetings are not held, since many colostomists who have surgery for extensive malignant disease have a limited life span, and regular depletion of such ostomists might have a depressing effect on the majority of colostomists who are cured and return to a normal life. A newsletter is sent out each year to people who have been contacted by the visitors, or who have applied for help by telephone or letter.

The *Urinary Conduit Association* is the most recently formed of the voluntary patient associations. It is rapidly increasing its membership and number of centres in the United Kingdom. The number of patients who have a urinary stoma is considerably smaller than those with an ileostomy or colostomy, but their need for help must be recognised. Meetings are held twice yearly and a visiting service is being built up in many areas.

Discussion of the work of the *Association for Spina Bifida and Hydrocephalus* (ASBAH) can be found in Chapter 9.

Mention must be made of the *International Ostomy Association* (IOA) to which most national patient organisations belong, and which has members in almost every country in the world; and the *World Council of Entero-Stomal Therapists* (WCET) which stoma care nurses practising in many countries have joined to share knowledge of stoma care on a world wide basis.

Companies manufacturing and supplying stomal equipment offer considerable help and expertise in the field of stoma care education. Many teaching aids are supplied or lent free of charge to medical and nursing schools, voluntary organisations and other people involved in stoma care. These include wall charts, tape-slide sets, films and booklets. Several firms also provide useful booklets for patients undergoing the various types of stoma surgery.

USEFUL ADDRESSES

Association for Spina Bifida and Hydrocephalus (ASBAH),
Tavistock House North,
Tavistock Square,
London WC1H 9HJ.
Tel: 01–388 1382/5

Colostomy Welfare Group,
38/39, Eccleston Square,
London SW1V 1PB.
Tel: 01–828 5175

Ileostomy Association of Great Britain and Ireland,
Amblehurst House,
Chobham,
Woking,
Surrey GU24 9PZ.
Tel: 09905–8277

Urinary Conduit Association,
Central Office,
36 York Road,
Denton,
Manchester M34 3HL
Tel: 061–336 8818

Sexual and Personal Relationship of the Disabled (SPOD),
25, Mortimer Street,
London W1N 8AB.
Tel: 01–637 5400

Chapter 18

The Role of the Nurse in Stoma Care

THE HOSPITAL OR COMMUNITY NURSE

The attitude of the nurse towards the giving of care to ostomists, either in a hospital situation or at home, plays a most important part in the progressive rehabilitation of this particular group of patients. It is regrettable that ignorance, and a lack of compassionate understanding on the part of the nurse, can sometimes do so much to undermine the already shaky morale of a stoma patient. The nurse is always regarded by the patient and his family as a trusted source of information and treatment. Her role is to reinforce this trust to the best of her knowledge and ability, though not to the extent of pretending to an expertise which she does not possess. It could be very damaging to a patient's psychological recovery to entrust the initial appliance change after surgery to a nurse totally inexperienced in stoma care.

The possibility of a nurse's uncontrolled reaction of revulsion to the stoma would certainly confirm the patient's own doubts and self-disgust, and probably lead to a protracted period of depression and lack of confidence.

The nurse in hospital or community will also be regarded by the other members of an ostomist's family as someone to whom they can refer for answers to the many questions which arise during the post-operative period, and this can pose considerable problems for nurses without any expert knowledge of stoma care.

Stoma patients require skilled individual treatment both pre-operatively and after surgery. It is unrealistic to assume that nurses working on busy surgical wards, where the available time has to be divided fairly between all the patients for whom they are responsible, will have either the opportunity or the specialised knowledge to provide this vital level of care and understanding. Similarly, the community nurse, with her heavy and varied case-load, cannot be expected to know details of the latest stoma equipment available, nor the solutions to the diverse problems, both practical and psychological, which may be encountered by the ostomist once he has returned home to his family.

It is hoped that some of the answers to these questions may be found between the covers of this book. Nurses in hospitals and the community who are involved in caring for stoma patients may now up-date their knowledge by attending one of the short courses in stoma care currently being offered in the United Kingdom. A certificate of attendance is awarded by the Joint Board of Clinical Nursing Studies to those nurses who complete the course successfully. The course runs from five to eight days and usually includes practical placements with qualified stoma care nurses in post, as well as covering both practical and psychological aspects of modern stoma care.

Although the subjects cannot be explored in depth in so short a time, these courses are of value as a source of topical information to nurses who seek to improve and consolidate their stoma care abilities.

THE STOMA CARE NURSE

The role of the stoma care nurse can be defined as that of a qualified, specialist resource person, trained in the practical management and care of all types of ostomist, and having the ability to recognise, evaluate and alleviate a variety of psychological difficulties which may occur after this type of surgery. The knowledge and expertise in all aspects of stoma care which such a specialist nurse must have requires a high level of academic ability, wide experience in practical nursing, and a compassionate dedication to furthering the rehabilitation of her patients.

The stoma care nurse does not confine her attention to any one age group or stratum of society, but applies her expertise to the care of all the stoma patients within her sphere, including those patients with fistulae or other drainage sites which require special treatment.

Stoma care begins when the stoma care nurse spends as much time as is necessary with every prospective stoma patient before surgery, giving and receiving information, and laying the foundations of a mutual trust and rapport which may well prove invaluable in the traumatic post-operative period. Close members of the patient's family may also be included at this time, so that they can have their questions answered and some of their fears allayed. It is of the utmost importance, at this stage, that both the patient and the family understand that there is a qualified nurse available to provide a specialised service, and that this will be an ongoing commitment covering all the aspects of life with a stoma, both in hospital and after returning home.

The stoma care nurse is an accessible source of information and practical guidance, part of the whole caring team; a communicator and not a dictator.

Close liaison between the ward sister or charge nurse and the stoma care nurse is absolutely essential. Mutual respect and co-operation should make for a pleasant and harmonious working relationship. Great tact and delicacy of approach may be necessary at times to obtain the ward sister's blessing for the stoma nurse's activities on the ward, and in no way must the ward sister's authority be usurped. The stoma care nurse in post will normally instigate and monitor the stoma care for post-operative patients on the ward, teaching the ward nurses the correct application and management of appliances, and ensuring that there is an adequate supply of the right equipment on the ward for each stoma patient. She will progressively instruct and encourage the patient towards managing his own stoma care, and make sure that the highest possible degree of self-sufficiency is attained before discharge home.

A comprehensive knowledge of appliances and accessories is vital to the implementation of the stoma care nurse's role, together with a full understanding of the effects of medication and diet on the stomal action. Skin care is another essential area of knowledge for the stoma care nurse, who will quite often be consulted by hospital staff when skin problems occur with patients other than ostomists.

For those patients who wish to irrigate their stomas, the stoma care nurse will instruct and demonstrate the correct procedure, always stressing the need for awareness of possible problems. Knowledge of the special needs of the ostomist undergoing radiotherapy or antitumour therapy is another aspect of the stoma care nurse's role.

Such a diversely specialised range of knowledge obviously requires an intensive form of training. Courses in stoma care have been established in the UK through the Joint Board of Clinical Nursing Studies, which ensures that the national standard laid down is maintained by means of regular monitoring. The in-depth eight week long course is for state-registered nurses of ward sister grade, who will expect to be employed as stoma care nurses after completing the course. Details of the stoma courses are available from the Joint Board of Clinical Nursing Studies.

The syllabus covers the diseases which may necessitate stoma surgery; the different types of stoma surgery; appliances and skin care aids; counselling and communication skills; research methodology, and other topics relevant to stoma care. There is a written examination and practical assessment, and those nurses completing the course successfully receive the Joint Board of Clinical Nursing Studies Certificate in Stoma Care.

The number of stoma care nurses in Great Britain is slowly growing, but the lack of financial resources common to most health authorities, and a somewhat negative attitude towards recognising the need for establishing new posts, is depriving stoma patients in certain areas of the specialised care which is their due.

The role of the stoma care nurse extends far beyond the bounds of the hospital ward or clinic. She will lecture to students in the schools of nursing, to family practitioners, health visitors, pharmacists and nurses in the community, and be prepared to go and talk to any other groups who may request information on stoma care.

The stoma care nurse will liaise with all people concerned with the welfare of any stoma patient as and when the need arises. The personnel involved may include nurses and doctors in hospital or community, medical social workers, retail and hospital pharmacists, local government officials, supplies departments, appliance manufacturers, nurse educators, and very many others (see Figure 18.1).

There are many other aspects of the stoma care nurse's complex role, which make it an almost unique blend of counsellor, clinical nurse, teacher, administrator and researcher, and a very high degree of self-motivation is an essential ingredient for success. The diversity of the role is not always understood by those whose original concept of a stoma care nurse is of someone whose activities are confined to the emptying or changing of stoma bags, and better understanding can only be achieved by better communication and education.

Through regular contact with the representatives of appliance manufacturers, and the setting up of carefully controlled trials of innovations in the field of stoma care, stoma care nurses play an important part in the progressive improvement and development of new equipment and aids for the ostomist. By phasing out inefficient and wasteful items, and by careful selection of the best and most widely suitable ostomy supplies, an up-to-date stock system may be introduced and a considerable amount of money saved.

Research projects undertaken by stoma care nurses and their colleagues have proved to be of great value and interest over the last

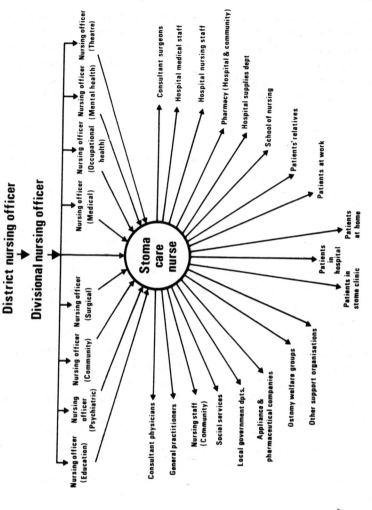

Figure 18.1 The stoma nurse's line of management and the contacts she makes. (From *Nursing Mirror Supplement*, June 8, 1978. Reproduced here by courtesy of *Nursing Mirror*.)

few years, and have helped to perpetuate an alive and forward-looking spirit amongst those nurses working with ostomy patients.

Perhaps the most important facet of the stoma care nurse's role, as far as the patient and family are concerned, is the maintenance after discharge home of the close contact established before and after surgery in hospital.

Community visits are made for as long as necessary, often in collaboration with the community nurse, and the patient is able to attend the stoma clinic for continuing contact and follow-up. Other stoma patients may be referred to the clinic by consultants, family practitioners, or community nurses. Patients can telephone the stoma care nurse personally and request assistance or information. This easy, informal access to help and reassurance is of immeasurable value to the patient who may have a problem, practical or psychological, but feels unsure and self-conscious about 'bothering the doctor'.

The main role of the stoma care nurse is to support the patient for as long as is necessary. It is important that all ostomists are made aware of the support available to them, and they should always be encouraged to seek help immediately a problem arises.

Stoma care is the giving of an individual service to an individual patient, the primary aim of which is to return that individual to the same place in society he occupied before surgery, and to rehabilitate him satisfactorily to the point where he feels able to take charge of his own destiny.

Stoma care is an exacting role, demanding skill and dedication of a very high order. If we, as stoma care nurses, can assist our patients towards achieving a quality of life acceptable both to them, as individuals, and to their families, our training and efforts will not have been wasted.

QUESTIONS FOR DISCUSSION

1) Discuss the role of the ward nurse in caring for stoma patients. How may her attitude affect their recovery and rehabilitation?
2) What means are available for nurses in the hospital and community to up-date their knowledge of stoma care?
3) Discuss the specialised range of knowledge and skills offered by a qualified stoma care nurse.
4) How may the stoma care nurse integrate with other members of the caring team?

5) By what means does the stoma care nurse fulfil her role as a teacher and communicator?

6) In your opinion, how could the role of the stoma care nurse be expanded further?

Index